NEW ENGLAND LIGHTHOUSES

BY BRUCE ROBERTS *and* RAY JONES

Southern Lighthouses
Chesapeake Bay to the Gulf of Mexico

Western Lighthouses
Olympic Peninsula to San Diego

Western Great Lakes Lighthouses
Michigan and Superior

Eastern Great Lakes Lighthouses
Ontario, Erie, and Huron

New England Lighthouses
Bay of Fundy to Long Island Sound

Mid-Atlantic Coast Lighthouses
Hudson River to Chesapeake Bay

New England
LIGHTHOUSES

BAY *of* FUNDY *to* LONG ISLAND SOUND

PHOTOGRAPHS *by* BRUCE ROBERTS
TEXT *by* RAY JONES

A Voyager Book

The Globe Pequot Press

Old Saybrook, Connecticut

Made by hand in Paris, France, during the nine-teenth century, Fresnel lenses worked by concentrating light into a tightly focused beam that could often be seen from dozens of miles away. The lenses came in a variety of sizes, or "orders." The sixth-order lenses were only seven-teen inches high with an inside diameter of less than a foot, while the huge first-order lenses stood nearly fifteen feet tall and had a diameter of more than six feet. The Boston Light has a second-order Fresnel lens about fourteen feet tall and sixty-six inches in diameter.

All photographs, unless otherwise credited, are by Bruce Roberts.
Editorial research by Cheryl Shelton-Roberts
Cover and text design by Nancy Freeborn

Library of Congress Cataloging-in-Publication Data
Roberts, Bruce.
    New England lighthouses : Bay of Fundy to Long Island Sound /
photographs by Bruce Roberts : text by Ray Jones. — 1st ed.
        p. cm. — (Lighthouses series)
        "A Voyager Book."
        Includes bibliographical references (p. 97) and index.
        ISBN 1-56440-944-9
        1. Lighthouses—New England. I. Jones, Ray. II. Title.
III. Series : Lighthouse series (Old Saybrook, Conn.)
VK1024.N38R625   1996
387.1'55'0974—dc20

96-18770
CIP

Front-cover photograph: Cape Elizabeth Light, Cape Elizabeth, Maine
Back-cover photograph: Pemaquid Point Light, Pemaquid Point, Maine

Printed in Québec, Canada
First Edition / 3RD Printing

To my daughter Lori

—*Bruce Roberts*

To George Worthylake, Ida Lewis, Dennis Dever, Lori Diggins,

Pat and John Remmers, and Edward Jones

—*Ray Jones*

With its classic lighthouse and romantic setting, Pemaquid Point reminds visitors of their intimate link to the sea.

ACKNOWLEDGMENTS

We sincerely appreciate the assistance of Coast Guard historians Robert L. Scheina, Dr. Robert Browning, Kenneth Arborgast, and other men and women of the U.S. Coast Guard; Ken Black of the Shore Village Museum in Rockport, Maine; Wayne Wheeler of the United States Lighthouse Society; William L. Trotter of the American Lighthouse Historical Society; Tim Harrison of *Lighthouse Digest;* Bill Kaufhold for his excellent photographs; Bob and Sandra Shanklin for theirs; Ben and Luanne Russell of Hendricks Head Lighthouse, Maine; The Rose Island Lighthouse Foundation, Rhode Island; Candace Clifford of the National Park Service Maritime Initiative, Washington, D.C.; and Lynn-Marie Richard, librarian of the Museum of the Atlantic in Halifax, Nova Scotia.

CONTENTS

Built in 1876 on the far southwestern tip of Cape Cod, the Nobska Lighthouse serves Woods Hole, Massachusetts, and its famed marine-research institute. Nobska's flashing light warns vessels away from a pair of vicious shoals, known locally as the Hedge Fence and L'Hommedieu.

INTRODUCTION

"No man is an island." So wrote John Donne, the often-quoted British poet and clergyman. But Donne, who died in 1631, never knew any of the lighthouse keepers who, for more than two centuries, helped make North America's coasts safe for navigation. For these brave men and women, life was an island. Surviving on subsistence-level government salaries, they lived mostly on wild headlands and treeless ledges very far from what most of us would call civilization. Often the closest town was itself a backwater, a remote outpost. Depending on the weather, even the nearest rural church might seem impossibly distant.

When bad weather rushed in from the ocean, as it often did, lighthouse keepers could not follow the example of the mariners they served and run for a calm harbor. Since their ships had stone foundations and no sails, rudders, or helms, they had to stay and take whatever the sea threw at them. To fight back against gale and gloom, they had only their lights, and whatever conditions, whatever the health of the keepers, these had to be kept burning. The lamps, which often stood at the top of winding staircases with hundreds of steps, were in constant need of attention. As a result, the keepers always worked nights and never had a day off.

Lighthouse keepers endured this sort of existence, not necessarily for any high-minded or romantic reason—for instance, because they loved the sea, the wind, the cold, or the isolation—but for the same reason that most people work: It rewarded them with a place to live and a smattering of pay. It was also a job worth doing, a job that had to be done.

RIVERS *in the* SEA

The waters just off the eastern coasts of the United States and Canada serve as a superhighway for ships. Two great rivers in the Atlantic, the cold Labrador Current flowing down from the north and the warm Gulf Stream sweeping up from the south, form the separate lanes of this highway. For centuries, all the way back to the time of the earliest explorers, mariners have used these swift-flowing currents to speed their ships back and forth from Europe.

Because the currents hug the coast, ships sailing in these natural sea-lanes are constantly at risk of running aground on shoals or smacking into some fog-shrouded headland. Sometimes ships slip into the wrong lane, where they may collide with another vessel sailing in the opposite direction. As a consequence of these dangers, the sandy sea bottom along the North American eastern coast has become a graveyard covered with the ribs of wrecked ships and the bones of unlucky seamen.

For more than two centuries, lighthouses have served as the "traffic cops" of this crowded and dangerous ocean highway, warning ships away from knife-edged rocks and guiding them safely to port. Dozens of red-hulled lightships also once provided guidance, but all of these have now been pulled off station and retired. According to the U.S. and Canadian Coast Guards, which maintain lighthouses, buoys, and other aids to navigation, the old lightships have simply outlived their usefulness.

But lighthouses remain vital to shipping, especially along the bustling U.S. Atlantic seaboard. The beacons of nearly 250 lighthouses form an almost continuous band of light along the thousands of miles of coastline between Brownsville, Texas, on the U.S.–Mexican border, and Cape Breton, on the far north-eastern tip of Nova Scotia. More than half of the total are located in New England or the Canadian Maritimes. The more historic and picturesque of these "northern lights" are the subjects of this book. So, too, are the brave men and women who have kept the lights burning through the centuries.

BOSTON LIGHTS *the* WAY

The first true lighthouse in North America was built on Little Brewster Island, at the entrance to Boston Harbor. George Worthylake, a shepherd and harbor pilot, climbed to the top of the newly completed tower on the evening of September 14, 1716. There, with the sun descending in the west and a blanket of darkness racing across the ocean from the east, Worthylake put a match to the light's tallow candles for the first time. On that night and the many thousands of nights since, the masters of ships headed for Boston have seen the light and known that safe water lay ahead. Mariners still see it today, almost three centuries after it first shined out over the harbor.

After the light on Little Brewster was established, Boston became a magnet to shipping, and merchants and warehousemen along the city's waterfront prospered. The new lighthouse proved far less profitable for Worthylake, however. Fate had no fortune in store for him. His salary of fifty pounds a year was supposed to be supplemented by fees for serving as harbor pilot. But Worthylake's responsibilities as keeper proved much more arduous and time-consuming than expected, and he had little time left over for piloting.

To help feed and clothe his family, the keeper ran herds of sheep on Little Brewster and other nearby islands, but Worthylake had no more luck as a shepherd than he did as a pilot. During a terrible winter gale in 1717, several dozen of his sheep wandered out onto a spit, where they were soon stranded by the tide. Since he could not in good conscience abandon his post in the midst of a storm, Worthylake could do nothing to assist these hapless animals. From the high lantern of the lighthouse, he watched in despair as one after another of his sheep washed off the spit and into the sea.

In all, Worthylake lost fifty-nine sheep to the storm. To help ease the financial burden of this loss, the town of Boston agreed to increase the keeper's salary to seventy pounds. Unfortunately, Worthlake never got to enjoy his new salary. As he was returning from Boston, where he had gone to collect his pay, his boat capsized only a hundred

This old fog bell saved many ships from disaster off Pemaquid Point in Maine.

yards or so from the safety of the dock on Little Brewster Island. The shepherd-turned-lighthouse keeper drowned, and his body washed ashore on the same spit where his sheep had perished. By the time his body was discovered, the money that he had received in Boston had mysteriously vanished.

Robert Saunders, the second Boston keeper, also drowned, only a few days after he took over the job. Undaunted by the misfortunes of his predecessors, Captain John Hayes replaced Saunders, and Hayes not only survived but managed to prosper during his fifteen-year stay on the island. So, too, did most of the nearly sixty other keepers who lived and served on Little Brewster after him.

Despite its ominous beginnings, lighthouse keeping would eventually become an honored and distinguished profession in North America. During the more than 280 years since George Worthylake first climbed the steps of Little Brewster Island tower, thousands of dedicated men and women have kept lights burning at hundreds of critical locations along the U.S. and Canadian coasts. They have saved countless lives, and, by making navigation safer and cheaper, they have helped to bring prosperity to the entire continent.

Unfortunately, the profession of lighthouse keeping is now all but extinct. Driven by budget cuts and demands for ever-greater efficiency, the U.S. and Canadian Coast Guards have automated one lighthouse after another. Technology has replaced the sharp eyes and strong, steady fingers of keepers with automatic timers, radio relays, and satellite transmissions. Although they continue the necessary work of marking dangerous obstacles and guiding vessels safely to port, our lighthouses now stand their vigils alone. For much of the last two and a half centuries, however, that was not the case. The lights could do their jobs only with the help of skilled human hands.

THE WORST SEA IS COMING

Keepers usually lived at lighthouses with their families, who faced the loneliness, hardship, danger, and punishing weather along with them. Family members often shared the heavy work of keeping the lights burning, frequently displaying the same heroic resolve as the keepers themselves. The following tale illustrates the hardiness and dedication of lighthouse families.

On a stormy night in 1856, young Abbie Burgess drew up a chair to the kitchen table at the battered keeper's residence on Matinicus Rock, Maine, and dipped her pen into ink. A lonely seventeen-year-old, separated by at least twenty-five miles of turbulent sea from the nearest barn dance, church social, or country store, she had decided to write a letter to a pen pal on the mainland:

> You have often expressed a desire to view the sea out on the ocean when it was angry. Had
> you been here on 19 January [1856], I surmise you would have been satisfied. Father was
> away. Early in the day, as the tide rose, the sea made a complete breach over the rock, wash-
> ing every movable thing away, and of the old dwelling not one stone was left upon another.
> The new dwelling was flooded, and the windows had to be secured to prevent the violence of
> the spray from breaking them in. As the tide came, the sea rose higher and higher, till the
> only endurable places were the light towers. If they stood, we were saved, otherwise our fate
> was only too certain. But for some reason, I know not why, I had no misgivings, and went on
> with my work as usual. For four weeks, owing to rough weather, no landing could be effected
> on the rock. During this time we were without assistance of any male member of our family.

Though at times greatly exhausted with my labors, not once did the lights fail. I was able to perform all my accustomed duties as well as my father's.

You know the hens are our only companions. Becoming convinced, as the gale increased, that unless they were brought into the house they would be lost, I said to my mother, "I must try to save them." She advised me not to attempt it. The thought, however, of parting with them without an effort was not to be endured, so seizing a basket, I ran out a few yards after the rollers had passed and the sea fell off a little, with the water knee deep, to the coop, and rescued all but one. It was the work of a moment, and I was back in the house with the door fastened, but I was none too quick, for at that instant my little sister, standing at the window, exclaimed, "Oh look! look there! The worst sea is coming." That wave destroyed the old dwelling and swept the rock. I cannot think you would enjoy remaining here any great length of time for the sea is never still and when agitated, its roar shuts out every other sound, even drowning our voices.

A few years after the extraordinary month-long Atlantic storm described in her letter, Abbie Burgess married a lighthouse keeper. She and her husband eventually became assistant keepers of the Matinicus Rock Light.

A BELL *in the* NIGHT

Of course, not all lighthouse stories end as happily as the one above. Several miles south of the Boston Light, Minots Ledge Lighthouse stands on a scrap of rock that disappears under the waves at each high tide. The tower usually cannot be made out from Little Brewster, but at night, unless the weather is especially heavy, its light can always be seen. The granite Minots tower is the second lighthouse built on the ledge. The first was an experimental structure, an iron skeleton with eight legs that stood with their feet in the ocean. In a raging storm in the early morning darkness of March 17, 1851, the experiment failed.

When the gale had set in the previous night, keeper John Bennett was on the mainland. The weather was so severe that he could not return to his post. This left the light in the hands of assistant keepers Joseph Antoine and Joseph Wilson, both close friends of Bennett. As the storm grew worse and titanic waves began to roll in out of the east, Bennett and other spectators on shore began to wonder if the lighthouse could possible stand up to the pounding. Their fears were well founded.

Shortly after one o'clock, the skeleton began to sag toward land. The tearful Bennett, who realized now that he would never again speak to his two friends, noted with bitter pride that somehow his assistants kept the light burning right down to the last instant. As the lantern room neared the water, just before the lighthouse collapsed and fell into the sea, the waves began to hit the station fog bell, causing it to ring out wildly.

CHAPTER ONE

Lights of
THE GRANITE HEADLANDS

NOVA SCOTIA, NEW BRUNSWICK, *and* EASTERN COAST *of* MAINE

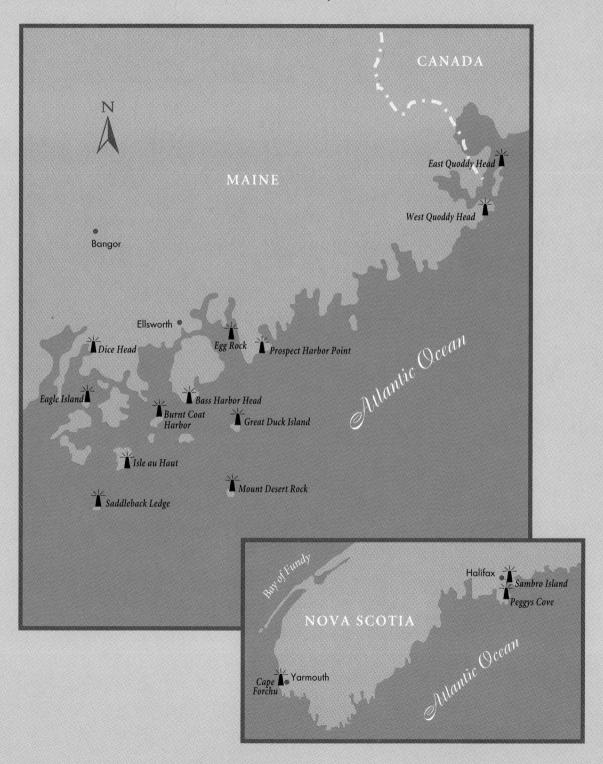

CANADA

MAINE

East Quoddy Head

West Quoddy Head

Bangor

Ellsworth

Dice Head

Egg Rock

Prospect Harbor Point

Atlantic Ocean

Eagle Island

Bass Harbor Head

Burnt Coat Harbor

Great Duck Island

Isle au Haut

Mount Desert Rock

Saddleback Ledge

Bay of Fundy

Halifax

Sambro Island

Peggys Cove

NOVA SCOTIA

Cape Forchu

Yarmouth

Atlantic Ocean

When the glaciers retreated more than 10,000 years ago, they left behind a rugged, rock-strewn coastline that makes Nova Scotia prime lighthouse country. The diminutive Peggys Cove tower is only one of dozens of lighthouses that warn mariners against the dangers of these treacherous yet photogenic shores. (Courtesy Chris Kelly)

*I*solation breeds eloquence. For proof of this, one need only turn to the logs and letters of lighthouse keepers. As members of a profession that paid them barely enough to live, these rugged, rawboned men and women were frugal in all things, even in their use of language. Nature and circumstance taught them to place a special value on words. Huddled together on roadless headlands or barren ledges far out in the sea, the keepers and their families soon ran out of small talk. They spoke only when they needed to speak, and even then, they whittled their sentences down to an efficient minimum. A thing had to be said and be done with; otherwise, the words blew away in the wind or drowned in the roar of the ocean.

Even so, some have counted lighthouse keepers among the world's best storytellers. Wordsmiths the likes of Daniel Webster and Henry David Thoreau have smoked pipes and sipped mugs of coffee with New England keepers and felt tingles running up their spines at stories of storm, shipwreck, sacrifice, and heroism. Thoreau especially admired the keeper's way of spinning a tale, not with miles of silk but with a few yards of good, stout yarn.

In the following passages, keepers tell what it was like to live in a lighthouse.

A REAL HUMMER

After the light itself, the chief concern of a lighthouse keeper was the weather. Probably no other profession ever exposed its members to worse in the way of climate. The keepers of island and ledge lights and caisson-style lighthouses built directly over the shoals they guarded were especially vulnerable to bad weather. In a gale a lighthouse, such as the one on Saddleback Ledge in the Penobscot Bay, Maine, is a ship without a helm. Unable to run for a safe harbor or duck into a quiet cove, it is a motionless obstacle standing directly in the path of a furious ocean.

Saddleback Ledge keeper W. W. Wells described one such angry sea to a fellow "Wickie," or lighthouse keeper:

> The storm struck in the dead of night, the wind blew a sixty-mile gale. With it came the seas. They struck plentiful and hard. I did not even dare to peek out the door to see what was doing. We had the shutters all closed on the windows so as not to break any glass. . . . One tremendous [sea that boarded us] seemed to shake us like a tablecloth. I thought it was going to clean up the works. Why it didn't I have never been able to fathom out. When the storm subsided, we ventured out to look things over.
>
> Things were certainly a mess. Over 128 feet of our boat slip was torn up, sink spout ripped away, and the cement breakwater built around the light to protect it, broken through in several places. It trimmed up our boathouse doors that were very strongly made. It threw a 140-gallon oil tank and boathouse door upon the winch hoist and put that out of commission. . . . It ripped the slopboards off on the east side of the house, and water came in from the roof where it had torn off the shingles. Take it altogether, it was a hummer.

NIGHT *of the* BIRDS

When it came to weather, keepers learned to expect the unexpected. They were usually prepared for gales that flew in off the ocean with little or no warning. But nature had other surprises in store—for instance, attacks by airborne armies of suicidal ducks. Wells told the following story to a friend:

We keepers were setting in the kitchen talking about the [First] World War when bang, bang, bang, something came against the windowpanes. We thought that another war had started that we had not heard about.

All at once I heard glass smash in the lantern, and with this I thought sure the enemy were trying to extinguish the light.

This was just around supper time and it lasted until near midnight. Darkness had come on and with it came all the evidence that we were going to get a Sou'easter. As the storm struck so did the cannonading. I could not help thinking that it was only fair to inform us of the attack that was about to be made. A war with Mexico and Japan seemed to be the last topic of conversation just before the unexpected arrived. But who wanted to blow up a friendly old lighthouse that always did good instead of harm, and which mariners who sailed their ships along the coast loved and respected. Crash! and a bird came sailing through a pane of glass, dropping at my feet.

He began fluttering around the floor with one wing broken, and his bill telescoped almost through his head. He did not live long. In came another and away went another windowpane. The phenomenon was repeated again and again until the birds began to pile up like a mound.

Just when I thought the cannonading had ceased, one big sea drake struck the plate glass in the tower lantern and came through without asking for a transfer. When he struck he broke up the works. Before he stopped he put out the light and broke prisms out of the lens. The bird weighed over ten pounds.

Saddleback in darkness, what would the people think on land and sea? Only those who live in lighthouses could realize what excitement it all caused. The keepers got right to work, first to get the light going and then to make repairs as fast as possible. It was not long before old Saddleback was throwing her beams again as if nothing had ever happened.

One of us went to step out in the gallery when a big sea duck reported with bayonet and charged so heavily as to knock one's feet out from under. There was no more taking any chances leaving the kitchen until continued silence told the keepers that the enemy had retreated. When all had quieted down it was a strange sight that the keepers were greeted with, for at the base of the tower was a tremendous heap of birds, some dead and others alive. Those that were just dazed and needed to recuperate we placed in the boathouse, and the next day they went on their way.

Saddleback Ledge, near Isle au Haut, Maine, is a bare scrap of rock exposed on all sides to the rush of the sea. A forty-two-foot, cone-shaped gray stone tower has stood on the ledge since 1839, its flashing white light warning sailors against collision with the rock and certain calamity. The Saddleback Ledge Lighthouse was automated in 1954, but until that time, it was continuously staffed by keepers who lived on the ledge for weeks at a time. The tower of Saddleback Ledge Lighthouse still clings to its exposed rock, all traces of dwellings and outbuildings swept away by wind, water, and time.

WRECK *on* MOUNT DESERT ROCK

Lighthouse keepers less frequently played host to dazed ducks than to half-drowned seamen. Since they lived on the most dangerous stretches of coast, keepers often witnessed calamitous wrecks and nearly as often helped drag survivors out of the surf. For shipwrecked sailors, a keeper might serve as rescuer, physician, and innkeeper.

A keeper on Mount Desert Rock, Maine, left the following record of the early twentieth-century wreck of the tug *Astral:*

> *It was on December 9th, 1902 at 5 o'clock in the morning that the second assistant keeper whose morning watch it was, called me saying "I think I heard a steamboat blow a blast of seven whistles as if in distress."*
>
> *I jumped out of bed and dressed as quickly as possible. The vapor was flying so high and densely that one could see hardly ten feet ahead. It was inky dark and blowing one of the worst gales I had seen since being in the service.*
>
> *The thermometer never had dropped so low during the thirteen years I had been on the Rock. The assistant had noticed that the sounds of the whistle came from the northeast and so we went in that direction. It was then high tide but we could, after a fashion, make out that there was some kind of steamer ashore on the northeast point; but as the big seas were running so mountain high it would have meant suicide for any of us to try to get out where she was.*
>
> *The seas were running through between the main rock and the outer point. I could see that no boat could live to get to the outer point and across the expanse of rough water. We called and called, trying to get an answer. Not hearing or seeing anything, we stayed where we were until we nearly froze to death. We could not stand the terrific cold air and simply had to get back to the station. We were chilled to the bones and could hardly speak when we got into the house.*
>
> *My wife had plenty of boiling water and a big pot of coffee ready to serve instantly. As soon was we got thawed out so we could handle our fingers we began getting down ropes and life preservers as near the wreck as we could. We were compelled to wait until the tide went down and then we got across to the outer point. We could then see that it was a large ocean tug with a barge in tow. The terrific blows that the sea was pounding on the craft would turn her almost completely over. Between the seas I was able to get a line to them and, one by one, we succeeded in rescuing seventeen men.*
>
> *There were eighteen in the crew but one was frozen to death before we could get him ashore. They were all more or less frozen, and badly at that. The second engineer of the tug had to be carried to the house, his limbs being useless. He was in terrible condition. . . . Well, after we got them all to the house we treated their frostbites and got them a hot breakfast. That night we doused them with quinine pills and hot lemonade for fear they might come down with bad colds and pneumonia might set in.*

SAMBRO ISLAND LIGHT

Halifax, Nova Scotia – 1758

On a wild and barren granite island near the entrance to Halifax Harbor stands one of Canada's foremost historic treasures. It is neither a dusty archaelogical dig nor a cold marble war memorial. Government leaders do not meet here—although seagulls and cormorants do occasionally use the place for a noisy gathering. This is a hardworking monument that still does its job of guiding ships and warning them away from dangerous rocks just as it has done for nearly two and a half centuries. It is nothing less than the oldest operational lighthouse in North America. (The original Boston Lighthouse was built much earlier but was blown up by the British in 1776.)

To put the age of the Sambro Island Lighthouse into perspective, consider that when the Canadian Confederation met in 1867, the light had already stood for 109 years. The lighthouse predates Captain James Cook's famous around-the-world voyage of exploration (1776–79) and the American Revolution (1775–83). It was built at the height of a global conflict known nowadays as the French and Indian War. Fighting in the late 1750s for dominion

The octagonal tower of Sambro Lighthouse, the oldest in Canada, rises more than 150 feet above the waters of the Atlantic. More than five feet thick at the base, the tower has kept watch over its barren granite island for nearly two and one-half centuries. (Courtesy Paul Franklin)

over an entire continent, Britian and France confronted each other primarily at sea, and, as is often the case with maritime wars, lighthouses played a role.

In 1734 the French had established Canada's first true lighthouse, at Louisbourg, on the far eastern end of what is now Nova Scotia. But its light would serve only a single generation of mariners. In 1758 British cannon leveled the French fortress at Louisbourg and blasted the light tower; nearly a century would pass before the lighthouse would be rebuilt.

Late in 1758 British colonists completed a lighthouse of their own, on Sambro Island, to guide ships in and out of Halifax Harbor. A few months after it went into service, British general James Wolfe boarded a warship at Halifax and set sail for Quebec. The gleaming beacon of the new lighthouse was the last he would ever see of Halifax. In 1759, on the Plains of Abraham, just outside the city walls of Quebec, General Wolfe fought a decisive battle with the French. Wolfe was killed, but the British won the battle and with it the war.

Since it was built during wartime, the Sambro Island tower was given fortresslike granite walls sixty feet high and more than five feet thick at the base. To raise the necessary funding for the project, the colonial government levied a stiff tax on one of the most popular and plentiful commodities available in this rough, maritime colony: "spirituous liquors." Construction costs were astoundingly high for the time—in excess of a thousand pounds sterling. But as it turned out, the people of Halifax got a bargain for their money. The Sambro Island Lighthouse has successfully stood up to storms that have swept away whole fishing villages along the Nova Scotia Atlantic coast. It has out-

lasted ten generations of keepers, and its light has shined on all but a very few of the last 88,000 nights.

Of course, there have been many changes at the station over the years. In 1906 a new twenty-foot section was added to the walls, giving the tower an overall height of eighty-two feet. With the seventy-foot height of the bubble-shaped granite island added in, the light now stood more than 150 feet above the sea. At the same time the old octagonal walls were encased in a protective covering of shingles and painted with broad red and white stripes to make the tower more distinctive.

Whale-oil lamps originally provided the light that beamed seaward from the lantern room at the top of the tower. Over the years, coal oil, kerosene, and a variety of other fuels have been used in the lamps. For much of this century, the light of electric lamps was focused by a huge, nine-foot tall, first-order Fresnel lens. In 1967 the big Fresnel was replaced by a powerful airport-style beacon, which still serves today. Its light can be seen from seventeen miles away.

But the biggest change at Sambro Island came when the lighthouse was automated in 1988. In March of that year, John Fairservice, the station's last keeper, stepped into a boat with his family and set out for Halifax. For the first time in 230 years, the old lighthouse was left to stand its nightly vigil alone. Halifax newspapers lamented that it was now "a light without a heart." But even with its keeper gone, the old lighthouse still has many friends. A number of provincial organizations, including the Nova Scotia Lighthouse Preservation Society, looks after its interests. The society is raising money to help maintain the lighthouse and restore the old gas house and other buildings at the station.

HOW TO GET THERE:

For information on summer tours of Sambro Island, write to the Nova Scotia Lighthouse Society, c/o Maritime Museum of the Atlantic, 1675 Lower Water Street, Halifax, B3J IS3, or call (902) 424–6442. In addition to many other fascinating exhibits and historic artifacts, the museum houses the enormous, first-order Fresnel lens removed from Sambro Island Lighthouse in 1967. The museum is located on the Halifax waterfront near the Tourist Bureau and ferry landing.

PEGGYS COVE LIGHT

Peggys Cove, Nova Scotia – 1868

Along the entire southern coast of Nova Scotia, a great natural seawall of incredibly old granite holds back the Atlantic. Here storm-driven waves crash into a jumble of giant stone blocks and boulders left over from the ice age. Where the granite wall now stands, there once soared a mile-high range of ice mountains, the leading edge of a continent-size glacier. When all of this ice melted, at the end of the last glacial epoch, more than 10,000 years ago, it left behind a scarred and fractured landscape. A sailor's nightmare of rugged peninsulas and headlands and long, narrow inlets with rocky shoals and tricky currents, Nova Scotia is prime lighthouse country.

To make navigation safer and guide ships to port, dozens of lights mark the coastline from Halifax southwestward to Cape Sable and northwestward to the Bay of Fundy. Among the better-known lighthouses in the vicinity of Halifax are Georges Island, Chebucto Head, McNabs Island, Devils Island, Peggys Cove, and Sambro Island—the oldest lighthouse in North America. Farther down the coast are the Lahave and Mosher Island lighthouses. And rounding the cape are the lights at Sandy Point, McNutt Island, Barrington, Baccaro Point, Cape Sable, Bon Portage, Seal Island, Woods Harbour, Pubnico, and Cape Forchu.

A full moon enhances the reputation of Peggys Cove Lighthouse as one of the prettiest and most frequently photographed man-made structures in Canada. The tower's perch is an outcropping of granite scrapped and rounded by glacial ice. (Courtesy Paul Franklin)

To honor these lights and the men and women who have kept them burning—in the case of Sambro, for more than two centuries—the main highway from Halifax to Yarmouth has been dubbed the "Lighthouse Route." Those who drive this highway—Nova Scotia Route 103—are sometimes disappointed by the lack of lighthouses along the main road. The lights are tucked away at the end of charming country roads that lead to the sea. Adventurous travelers who turn off these often bucolic byways are likely to be well rewarded. For instance, Route 333 runs southward along the extraordinarily beautiful shoreline of St. Margarets Bay to the picture-postcard village of Peggys Cove.

During the summer, Peggys Cove is awash in tourists who come here to enjoy the ocean scenery, walk through the quaint fishing village, and visit the old lighthouse. Topped by a red metal lantern, the octagonal masonry tower is painted white and stands only thirty-seven feet tall. Although hardly among Canada's most impressive lighthouses, the little tower has a spectacular setting. Rising from an outcropping of waveswept granite, it is surrounded by boulders nearly as big as the tower itself. The rocks hereabouts are among the oldest—nearly 400 million years—on the planet.

Built in 1868, Peggys Cove Lighthouse guided fishermen and other mariners for more than a century before being discontinued by the Canadian Coast Guard. It serves today as a centerpiece for one of the loveliest and most popular coastal villages in North America.

In addition to its lighthouse, Peggys Cove is known for the enormous, hundred-foot-wide granite fishermen's memorial, sculpted by the late William de Garth. Depicting a party of thirty fishermen at work, the sculpture celebrates a way of life that has now all but vanished.

The lighthouse remains the most popular attraction at Peggys Cove. Those who photograph the tower and stand beside it to enjoy the view, however, should not forget that the structure once served a deadly serious purpose. During its long career its light no doubt saved many ships and countless lives. But it could not prevent one of the worst maritime disasters in Canadian history, which took place near here in 1873, only five years after the light at Peggys Cove went into service. Apparently misreading the light and other navigational markers in the area, the helmsman of the SS *Atlantic* steered the passenger liner into nearby Meaghers Rock. The *Atlantic* quickly sank, taking 562 pas-

Peggys Cove Light stands on bedrock that has defied the angry seas for eons. (Courtesy William Kaufhold)

sengers and crew with her. More than 270 victims of the disaster are buried in a cemetery at Prospect, a few miles to the east.

Some say that Peggys Cove got its name from an earlier shipwreck, when a schooner ran aground here and sank. The only survivor, a young woman called Peggy, married a local fisherman and so gave the place its name. A much more likely explanation is that the cove, located at the entrance to St. Margarets Bay, was named after that "Peggy" instead.

HOW TO GET THERE:

About 15 miles west of Halifax on Route 103, take exit 2 and turn south onto Route 333. Drive about 12 miles alongside scenic St. Margarets Bay to Peggys Cove.

CAPE FORCHU LIGHT

Yarmouth, Nova Scotia – 1840 and 1962

When he sailed past the southern tip of what is now Nova Scotia in 1604, the French explorer Samuel de Champlain noted in his logbook a broken, rocky headland pointing threateningly toward the sea. Champlain called this place Cape Forchu, or "Forked Cape." Over the centuries since then, the cape has lived up to its ominous name by repeatedly thrusting its jagged tines into the hulls of ships. It is especially dangerous when covered by one of the dense blankets of fog that frequently roll in off the Atlantic.

To help sailors avoid the cape's ship-killing rocks and guide them safely into nearby Yarmouth Harbour, a lighthouse was established on the cape in 1840. An octagonal wood-frame structure, it was one of the first lighthouses in North America to employ an advanced Fresnel lens. Manufactured in France, the Cape Forchu lens consisted of 360 separate prisms, weighing a combined 3,300 pounds. The lens had eight bull's-eyes, which concentrated light into narrow beams. Mariners saw these beams in a series of flashes as the lens rotated. The heavy lens floated in a pool of mercury, its rotation driven by a clockwork mechanism powered by heavy weights. The keeper or an assistant had to climb to the top of the tower six times each night to raise the weights. Herbert Cunningham, who served as keeper here from 1922 to 1952, said that he climbed the tower steps more than 47,000 times.

The airport-style lens of today's Cape Forchu Lighthouse requires no winding—in fact, in needs very little maintenance of any kind. The old Fresnel was removed and placed in a museum when the original tower was torn down and replaced in 1962. An inverted, hexagonal pedestal, the new tower is disconcertingly modern in appearance; it has been nicknamed the "Apple Core" by some of the more tradition-minded local folk. It nonetheless does its job quite efficiently, as its two-million-candlepower beacon can be seen from up to thirty miles at sea.

HOW TO GET THERE:

The Cape Forchu Lighthouse is often the first sign of Nova Scotia seen by visitors approaching Yarmouth by ferry from Maine. To reach the lighthouse from the ferry landing in the center of town, go north on Main Street, turn left onto Vancouver Street, then turn left again onto Route 304. In Overton, turn left at the sign for Cape Forchu. The lighthouse stands at the end of the road. Yarmouth offers plenty of interesting shopping and turn-of-the-century charm. The Yarmouth County Museum, at 22 Collins Street, just off Main Street, houses the original Fresnel lens from the old Cape Forchu Lighthouse. The Marine Atlantic (Blue Nose) Ferry service from Bar Harbor, Maine, to Yarmouth currently runs only during the summer months. For information on ferry schedules and attractions in Yarmouth and Nova Scotia, call (800) 341–7981 or (207) 288–3395.

The Cape Forchu Lighthouse is sometimes referred to unpoetically as "the Apple Core." (© James Steeves/Atlantic Stock Images Inc.)

EAST QUODDY HEAD LIGHT

Campobello Island, New Brunswick – 1830

Franklin D. and Eleanor Roosevelt maintained a thirty-four-room "cottage" on Campobello Island, where they spent many pleasant summers. It is easy to imagine the Roosevelts scrambling over the rocks to picnic within sight of the huge red cross that distinguishes the East Quoddy Head Lighthouse tower. Such an outing would not have been possible, however, after Franklin Roosevelt was stricken with polio. His first symptoms appeared while he was on holiday with his family at Campobello. Some say that Roosevelt may have contracted the dread disease while swimming in the nearby St. Johns River. Although crippled for life, Roosevelt went on to win election as governor of New York and to serve an unprecedented three full terms and part of a fourth as the nation's president during a crucial period of U.S. history.

East Quoddy Head Light, also known as Head Harbour Light, is located at the northern end of Campobello Island in New Brunswick. It stands approximately sixteen miles from the Roosevelt cottage and about eighteen miles from the international bridge linking the island to Lubec, Maine. Like a flock of gulls perched on a rock beside the sea, the white tower and outbuildings cluster together on a rugged and utterly barren headland.

The buildings and much of the octagonal tower are of wood construction. The roofs of the buildings and the lantern atop the tower are all painted red. The large red cross on the side of the tower, a typical marking for Canadian lighthouses, is said to make the station easier to see when the headland is covered by snow. The lantern displays a fixed red light intended to warn ships away from the headland's jagged rocks.

HOW TO GET THERE:

To reach this unusually scenic light, you must cross the international bridge at the end of Route 189 in Lubec, Maine. Customs officials there may suggest that you register your camera equipment before entering Canada. Roughly 2 miles from the bridge, you will pass the Roosevelt cottage, which is maintained by the Canadian government as the chief attraction of Roosevelt Park. If American history or the Roosevelt family interests you, then plan to spend an afternoon there. About a mile beyond the cottage, take a right at an unmarked intersection and continue for approximately 15 miles. The last 3 miles of the road are dirt.

The lighthouse tower, outbuildings, and grounds are all closed to the public and are difficult to see from the parking area. But you can get an excellent view by climbing down an iron ladder, crossing a gray pebble beach, and then climbing up another metal ladder to the summit of the cliff on the opposite side. Beware! The rungs of the ladders are very slippery, as are the algae-covered rocks below them. Unless you are cautious and surefooted, you may end up on a stretcher. Also, keep a close eye on the water level. The tides here rise at the incredible rate of 5 feet per hour and may very well cover the connecting beach while you are out enjoying the spectacle of the East Quoddy Head Light and the ocean. If this should happen, you will be most unhappily trapped on the rocks without amenities for at least eight hours. Don't count on the Canadian Mounties or Coast Guard for rescue.

On your way back to the United States, notice the discontinued Mulholland Light. It stands just across the narrows from Lubec and can be seen on your right as you drive back over the international bridge toward U.S. soil.

Displaying the red-cross design seen on many other Canadian lighthouses, East Quoddy Head Light warns sailors away from this treacherous headland with a red beacon. Tides here can rise at the incredible rate of five feet per hour.

WEST QUODDY HEAD LIGHT

West Quoddy Head, Maine – 1808 and 1858

The name of this light is ironic, since the tower stands on the easternmost point of land in the United States. Situated on a forty-foot-high cliff, the light overlooks Quoddy Narrows, which separates the United States from Canada. Across this channel lies Campobello Island, with East Quoddy Head at its northeastern end; hence the name West Quoddy Head for the American light.

West Quoddy is among the oldest lights in Maine. Throughout the early years of the nineteenth century, cit-

izens, merchants, and mariners operating out of the port of Passamaquoddy demanded that a lighthouse be placed on West Quoddy Head. "We . . . take the liberty to suggest that the site [West Quoddy] on the mainland bank being forty feet above the water is the most projecting . . . and judicious that can be pitched upon for that purpose," they told their government.

By 1806 President Thomas Jefferson was convinced of the need and signed an order for construction of a light-

Red stripes distinguish West Quoddy Head Lighthouse, which, despite its name, stands on the easternmost point in the United States. The weather here is often violent. Patches of artic tundra exist within a few yards of the tower.

house. By the end of the summer of 1808, all was in readiness, and keeper Thomas Dexter lit the first wicks in the lantern, some ninety feet above sea level. According to early charts and guides, the light could be seen in clear weather from a distance of seven leagues (about three miles) at sea.

Dexter's pay was set at an unprincely $250 per year. Being a family man, Dexter soon discovered that he could not live on this paltry salary. He complained to his employers at the U.S. Treasury Department that the soil at West Quoddy was too poor for gardening and that he had to travel a considerable distance to purchase supplies. Dexter's government bosses must have had families themselves; mindful of his plight, they increased his salary—to $300 per year.

Among the chief worries of shipmasters passing near West Quoddy Head and its knife-edged Sail Rocks were the thick banks of fog that frequently billowed up out of the nearby Bay of Fundy. More than one ship got lost in the fog and came to grief on the rocks. To warn ships of the danger, a 500-pound bell was installed at the light station in 1820. During foggy weather the keeper rang the bell at regular intervals, for which service he was paid an additional $70 per year. Unfortunately, mariners often could not hear the bell until they were far too close to the treacherous rocks. The station experimented with a high-pitched, 241-pound bell, a deeper-throated 1,500-pounder, and finally, a huge triangular steel bar some fourteen feet in length. But none of the bells proved satisfactory.

In 1837 lighthouse inspector Captain Joseph Smith sailed past West Quoddy Head on the revenue cutter *Morris,* and it seems that he himself got lost in the fog. Smith later wrote a report that said that the station needed "a sharp-toned bell of some 4,000 pounds weight." Apparently, Smith did not trust lighthouse keepers because he called for the bell to be "struck by machinery." Today West Quoddy Head has a powerful foghorn activated by a robotic fog-sensing device.

On orders from the Lighthouse Board, the tower was pulled down and completely reconstructed in 1858. The new tower rises eighty-five feet above the sea and was painted with showy red-and-white stripes for better daytime visibility. This tower still stands today, its third-order Fresnel lens displaying a pair of two-second flashes four times each minute.

HOW TO GET THERE:

From U.S. 1, turn toward Lubec on Route 189. After approximately 10 miles, turn right onto the road to Quoddy Head State Park and follow it for 5 miles to the lighthouse parking area. This is as far east as you can drive in the continental United States.

The lighthouse grounds are open to the public, but the tower and outbuildings are not. Both the lighthouse grounds and Quoddy Head State Park are closed at night and in winter.

The view here is spectacular. Cliffs drop down 40 feet or more onto a stony beach, while 100 yards or so offshore, waves crash over the Sail Rocks, which have torn through the hulls of many wooden sailing vessels. On the ocean horizon to the south lies Canada's enormous Grand Manan Island.

Take time to enjoy the state park nature trails, which feature patches of true arctic tundra more often seen thousands of miles to the north. Among the cobblestones on the beach you occasionally may find rounded bricks, worn and shaped by the surf. These may be left over from the old 1808 lighthouse, which was demolished in 1858.

On the drive back toward Route 189, you can see the Lubec Channel Light rising out of the water on your right. Built in 1890, this white conical tower stands on a black cylindrical pier and is completely surrounded by the waters of the Lubec Channel. Because of their unusual shape, lighthouses of this type are often called "spark-plug lights."

PROSPECT HARBOR POINT LIGHT

Prospect Harbor, Maine – 1850 and 1891

For more than a century, fisherman have put to sea nearly every morning from Prospect Harbor. This small village remains one of the last strongholds of an old-time way of life that is under siege or has been entirely displaced elsewhere. Lobster and sardine fishermen still live here, and each evening they are guided back home from the sea by the Prospect Harbor Point Light.

The light serves as a harbor marker and also warns boaters and fishermen away from the sharp, rocky protrusion of Prospect Point. The lantern displays a red light with two white flashes every six seconds. The light was left unstaffed after its last keeper, Captain Albion Faulkinham, retired in 1934.

Prospect Harbor had long been recognized as one of Maine's best anchorages when a light was finally placed here in 1850. The station was completely rebuilt and updated in 1891 on orders of the Lighthouse Board, but it has changed little in appearance since that time. Today the station is part of a military base. The keeper's cottage is used as a guest house for the base.

HOW TO GET THERE:

From U.S. 1, turn south onto Route 195 or Route 186. A few miles' drive on either road will bring you to Prospect Harbor village. A side road near the intersection of Routes 186 and 195 will take you within a few hundred feet of the lighthouse. Since the light station is located on an active military base, it is closed to the public. But you can park beside the road and walk out onto the red rocks leading down to the sea.

Prospect Harbor Light guides lobster and sardine fishermen safely back to port each evening. The station is now part of a military base, and astronauts have rested from their adventures in the adjacent keeper's dwelling.

EGG ROCK LIGHT

Frenchman Bay, Maine – 1875

Located on a massive gray ledge at the entrance of Frenchman Bay, this light marks the seaward approaches to Bar Harbor, gateway to Acadia National Park. The ledge itself is utterly barren. Since the last lighthouse keeper left in 1966, it has been inhabited only by seals and seabirds. Many birds choose to make their nests on the isolated ledge. Perhaps that is how Egg Rock got its name.

Built in 1875 on the order of President Ulysses S. Grant, the station consists of a stubby tower perched atop a square keeper's house. This squat structure is certainly not among the more attractive lighthouses in New England. The Coast Guard further marred its looks by removing the lantern room and replacing the old prism lens with an airport-type beacon. Purists were not above referring to Egg Rock Light as the "ugliest lighthouse in Maine." The Coast Guard recently reinstalled the lantern and restored the light to its original appearance.

Its looks do nothing to diminish its effectiveness, however, or the romance associated with it, as with all lighthouses. Millions of visitors to Acadia Park have seen and enjoyed its red flashing light reaching out across Frenchman Bay. Egg Rock Light has been described as a "pillar of fire in the Atlantic."

Cruise-ship captains are always glad to see the light; so long as they have it in view, the dangers of Egg Rock ledge can easily be avoided. Inbound pleasure boaters are also happy to see the light. Once they sight it, they know that not far ahead lies a delightful anchorage at Bar Harbor and a boiled-lobster dinner.

HOW TO GET THERE:

Take Route 3 from Ellsworth to Acadia National Park. The light can probably best be viewed from one of the scenic overlooks on the road through the eastern side of the park. But a particularly spectacular view of Egg Rock Light and of other lighthouses in the area can be had from the summit of 1,530-foot Cadillac Mountain. The parking lot at the top of the mountain is closed after dark, but you can usually stay to see the light come on at Egg Rock.

You should plan to remain in the area long enough to enjoy the natural scenic wonders of Acadia as well as the shops and restaurants in Bar Harbor. Also, don't miss the elegant afternoon tea served each day at the Jordan Pond House inside the park. A longtime favorite of park visitors, the tea features hot popovers and jam and can be enjoyed at outdoor tables overlooking Jordan Lake.

BASS HARBOR HEAD LIGHT

Mount Desert Island, Maine – 1858

Among the most picturesque lighthouses anywhere, Bass Harbor Head Light is seen and photographed each year by countless thousands of visitors to Acadia National Park. Clinging to a rocky promontory, the structure consists of a small white tower attached to a modest dwelling.

Established by the Lighthouse Board in 1858, during the presidency of James Buchanan, the light marked the entrance to Blue Hill Bay, on the west side of Mount Desert Island. It also assisted vessels moving in and out of Bass Harbor. The lighthouse continues to provide these same services to mariners today. Fishermen and pleasure boaters keep an eye out for its red light, which occults briefly every four seconds. (Occulting lights show longer periods of light than of darkness. Early occulting lights were often mechanically eclipsed so that they appear to blink on and off.)

Rocks in the vicinity of Bass Harbor Head show signs of scouring by ice. The same glacial forces that transformed the Maine coast into a maze of inlets and promontories also carved deep channels into stony Mount Desert Island. Not far to the north of the lighthouse is a geological wonder seen nowhere else in America—a fjord. Much like the well-known fjords of Norway, Mount Desert's Somes Sound is long, narrow, and walled in by steep cliffs. Sculpted from solid rock by a glacier, Somes Sound is a testament to the power of moving ice.

HOW TO GET THERE:

From Ellsworth, drive toward Acadia National Park on Route 3. Shortly after crossing over to Mount Desert Island, turn right onto Route 198. Turn right again onto Route 102 at Somesville, where you can get a look at Somes Sound, the only true fjord in the United States. Drive past Echo Lake and through the village of Southwest Harbor, a wonderful place for shopping and dining. Just beyond Bass Harbor a dirt road leads to the lighthouse parking lot. For more information, contact Acadia National Park at (207) 288–3338.

For lobster lovers: The best meals are not always to be had at fancy restaurants. Several roadside stands in this area offer boiled lobster and corn on the cob at bargain prices.

GREAT DUCK ISLAND LIGHT

South of Bass Harbor, Maine – 1890

Great Duck Island lies in the open Atlantic more than five miles to the south of Bass harbor. The lighthouse on the island was recently automated, but for nearly a century, it was staffed by up to four keepers, who usually housed their families with them there. These families lived for weeks and even months at a stretch with little or no contact with the mainland.

Rough weather often prevented the delivery of mail for weeks at a time. When the wind stopped howling, the ocean calmed, and the mail boat could put to sea to make its deliveries, the Great Duck keepers would receive several bushel baskets of letters, magazines, and outdated newspapers.

Keepers used to tell the story of a horrible wreck during a harsh winter gale. An entire crew was lost when its ship slammed into the rocks on the northeast side of the island. The keepers found only two bodies, a pair of sailors locked together in a grisly, frozen embrace. Since travel to the mainland was impossible, the two were buried in a common grave on the island. The ground was frozen so hard that the keepers had to use picks to dig the grave. For many years keepers maintained a tradition of laying a wreath each Memorial Day on the grave of the frozen sailors.

Flashing once every ten seconds, the red Great Duck Island Light helps mariners avoid most such encounters with the island's deadly rocks.

HOW TO GET THERE:

Neither the forty-two-foot tower nor its red light, flashing from sixty-seven feet above the sea, can be seen easily from land. They are best viewed from the air or from a boat passing on the south side of the island.

Named from the mighty flocks of waterfowl that gathered here until hunters decimated them, Great Duck Island is a lonely outpost. No one lives here now, but the island once had a thriving school for the children of lighthouse keepers. The Nature Conservancy maintains a wildlife preserve on the island.

MOUNT DESERT ROCK LIGHT

Mount Desert Rock, Maine – 1830, 1857, and 1893

On a rare calm December day shortly before Christmas in 1977, a helicopter settled onto the landing pad at Mount Desert Rock, some twenty-six miles out in the Atlantic Ocean off the Maine coast. A pair of eager young Coast Guardsmen, Robin Runnels, twenty-two, of Hyannis, Massachusetts, and Douglas Nute, twenty, of St. Louis, Missouri, tossed their gear into the chopper, hopped aboard, and strapped themselves in. They were more than ready to go. As the chopper lifted off and sped them on their way toward a welcome holiday with their families, the pair took full advantage of a gull's-eye view of the light station that would never again be their home. After the holidays they would take on new assignments somewhere far from the isolation of Mount Desert Rock. And the old lighthouse, its light and foghorn now fully automated, would continue to do its job—alone.

Runnels and Nute are the last names on a long list of keepers who have served time on "the rock," surely among the loneliest of the Coast Guard light stations. If the Great Duck Island (see page 23) keepers thought they were isolated, those on Mount Desert Rock must have felt like they were serving on the moon. An exceptionally dangerous obstacle for shipping, Mount Desert Rock is, indeed, little more than a rock. An open ocean ledge, it measures only 600 yards by 200 yards, and its highest point stands only twenty feet above the play of the sea.

Hardly anything grows naturally on the rock. Traditionally, lobstermen and other friends of the keepers brought baskets of soil to the station each spring. The keepers spread the dirt near the lighthouse or stuffed it into rain-moistened cracks and crevasses so that they would have a place to plant a garden and grow a few flowers. Usually, before the growing season was over, a stormy sea would rise up and wash away the blooms, the vegetables, and the soil, leaving behind only the bare rock.

The first lighthouse erected here in 1830 was a two-story cottage with a lantern set on its roof. This arrangement placed the light at a point fifty-six feet above mean sea level, not high enough to serve properly the heavy shipping traffic in these waters. When the Lighthouse Board was formed by act of Congress in 1851, one of its first actions was to authorize $10,000 for renovation of the light station at Mount Desert Rock. Because of the station's remote location, the work took several years to complete, but by 1857 a stone tower had raised the light slightly, to a height of sixty feet. Even with a powerful third-order Fresnel lens installed in the lantern, however, the light was still thought to be inadequate. Some decades later, in 1893, the tower was rebuilt, this time raising the light to seventy-five feet above the sea. The new granite tower had a broad base and walls as thick as those of a fortress to help it withstand angry seas.

Although the light was effective, it could not prevent the ocean tug *Astral* from slamming into Mount Desert Rock shortly before dawn on December 9, 1902. Despite sub-zero temperatures, the station's keepers managed to save all but one member of the tug's "more or less frozen" eighteen-man crew (see page 10).

HOW TO GET THERE:

While neither the lighthouse nor the ledge it stands on can be seen from shore, the light, flashing white at fifteen-second intervals, is a welcome sight for boaters and sailors in the area. The lighthouse also can be seen from the air. Small planes can be chartered at Bar Harbor Airport on Route 3.

Located twenty-six miles out in the Atlantic, Mount Desert Rock ranks among the nation's most isolated lighthouses. The station served for almost 150 years as a lonely home to keepers and their families before the light was automated in 1977. (Courtesy U.S. Coast Guard)

BURNT COAT HARBOR
(HOCKAMOCK HEAD) LIGHT
Swans Island, Maine – 1872

Why the name Burnt Coat? During the early seventeenth century, a great fire consumed much of the dense forest and other growth on what is today known as Swans Island. A party of French sailors who briefly visited the charred and inhospitable island supposedly gave it the name *Brun Côte,* or "Brown Coast." Since the French words easily twisted the tongues of later English-speaking settlers, the name became Burnt Coat.

Another, equally plausible, explantation for the name may lie with the island's first permanent resident, Thomas Kench. Driven half mad by the violence of the American Revolution, Kench deserted the Continental Army in 1776 and escaped to this remote place, where he lived as a hermit, far from the drums and destruction of war. As a deserter, he was said to have "burned his coat" or uniform: hence the name.

A squatter, Kench lived alone on the nine-square-mile island for more than a decade, but his peace and solitude could not last forever. Imagine Kench's dismay when his former commanding officer, Colonel James Swan, showed up and bought the island out from under him. One of the original Sons of Liberty, Swan had participated in the Boston Tea Party in 1773 and fought hard against the British during the Revolutionary War. But having helped rid the country of a king, Swan quickly grew tired of democracy and decided to carve out a kingdom of his own in the coastal north. Swan's royal aspirations proved financially ruinous, however, and he ended his days in a debtors' prison in Paris.

But Swans Island crowned another "king" with the arrival of David Smith. A strong-willed man, known to friend and foe alike as "King David," Smith took it upon himself single-handedly to populate the island. He eventually fathered twenty-four children, who further increased his tribe with more than fifty grandchildren. Smith's descendents have lived on the island for two centuries and have watched vessel after vessel pile up on the ship-killing ledges near Burnt Coat Harbor.

Burnt Coat appears a tempting refuge to a sea captain caught in a storm, but all too often, a ship making a run for the harbor ends up on the rocks. In 1872 the Lighthouse Board tried to help by building a pair of towers intended to serve as range lights. As with range lights elsewhere, the towers were built some distance apart, with the rear lantern at a greater elevation. Mariners who saw the lights lined up one atop the other were supposedly in a safe channel. Unfortunately, this arrangement tended to confuse local sailors, and wrecks occurred at an even faster pace than before. So, in 1885 the board decided to simplify matters by pulling down the smaller of the two lighthouses. The second lighthouse, on Hockamock Head, at the mouth of the harbor, still stands. Perched on a square tower forty-seven feet above the water, the lantern displays a green light occulting briefly every four seconds.

Despite the presence of the light, ships continued over the years to slam into the Swans Island rocks. As a result, the islanders have made an industry out of emptying the hulls of wrecked vessels. They have salvaged lumber, coal, and all sorts of other freight. Of course, they have found some cargoes more useful than others. On January 27,

HOW TO GET THERE:

Although situated several miles from the mainland, Swans Island can be reached via a car ferry operating daily out of Bass Harbor on Mount Desert Island. The ferry makes six round trips each day during the summer and four each day during the off-season. For schedule information and reservations, call the Maine Ferry Service at (207) 244–3254. Unless you are traveling in July and August, you should take food and drink with you. Very few businesses on Swans Island are open during the off-season.

A few miles north of Swans Island stands the Blue Hill Bay Lighthouse, on a scrap of ground with the well-chosen name of Fly Island. The island is quite low, and most of it disappears at high tide. The squat tower is no taller than the attached one-and-a-half-story keeper's dwelling. The lantern displays a green light that flashes once every four seconds.

1888, a certain Captain Brett at the helm of a fine schooner tried to duck out of a squall into the calm water of Burnt Coat Harbor. Unable to see in the thick weather, he missed the harbor altogether and ran up onto the stony shore. Brett and all six members of his crew escaped the disaster without injury—but not so the people of Swans Island. Following the storm, they gathered at the site of the wreck expecting to benefit from the salvage of a large cargo. They discovered, however, that the schooner holds were loaded to the hatches with turnips. No doubt the dogged salvagers ate turnips every day until nobody on the island could ever again stand the sight of the things.

This square-towered lighthouse on Hockamock Head marks the entrance to Burnt Coat Harbor on Swans Island. Weary of democracy, former patriot and Revolutionary War soldier James Swan tried, but failed, to carve out a kingdom for himself on this island during the late 1700s.

ISLE AU HAUT LIGHT

Isle au Haut, Maine – 1907

A gleaming white cylinder set on a tall base of rough-cut granite, this lighthouse is as lovely as it is unique. The same might be said of the pristine island on which the lighthouse stands. Its densely forested hills soar hundreds of feet above the Atlantic. Along with the mountains of Mount Desert Island, they are often the first land spotted by mariners sailing northwestward out of the Atlantic. In 1604 the French explorer Samuel de Champlain saw these heights rising blue above the ocean horizon and, landing on the island, found it delightful. Later, in a book about his explorations and adventures, Champlain described the place as "high and striking" and gave it the name *Isle Haute,* or "high island." Today it is known as Isle au Haut.

The people of Isle au Haut have always been an enterprising breed. During the early 1800s they fished, raised sheep, and operated a thriving saltworks. Meanwhile, sea captains from Isle au Haut sailed halfway around the world in their fast clipper ships to trade with China. By 1860 watermen here were canning their own lobster meat and selling it to London's Crosse & Blackwell. Later they helped create a new dining tradition in New York City by sailing for Manhattan each week with a cargo of hundreds of live Maine lobsters.

Although the rich waters around Isle au Haut continue to yield bounteous catches of lobster, most island residents

HOW TO GET THERE:

The island is served year-round by a ferry operating out of Stonington, on Deer Island. To reach Stonington, turn off U.S. 1 near the village of Orland and follow Route 15 for approximately 40 miles. Route 15 will carry you through some of the Earth's most lovely countryside and through Blue Hill, one of Maine's most attractive country towns. The Blue Hill Fair, held each year in September, was the model for the fair in Charlotte's Web, E. B. White's well-known children's novel. From Blue Hill, a brief side trip on Routes 172 and 175 will bring you to Blue Hill Falls, a tumbling rapid that reverses direction with the tides. A working fishing village, Stonington itself is worth the drive. Ferry hours vary with the season. For schedules and reservations, call (207) 367–2468.

now make their living from the tourist trade. In recent decades the year-round population has dropped to only a few dozen, but the island is crowded in July and August. As in communities throughout coastal Maine, many of the fine old homes on Isle au Haut are boarded up most of the year but are filled with light and laughter during the summer. An offshore extension of Acadia National Park, which takes up more than half of the island, attracts plenty of hikers and campers from the mainland.

But even in the summer, Isle au Haut remains a quiet retreat. The island has kept much of its rustic, old-time atmosphere. Most houses still have no electricity, so visitors must read their sea stories or *Down East* magazines by gaslight. It was only a few years ago that residents finally gave up on their antique, "Grandma Bell" telephone system—with the last operating crank-style telephones in the nation.

The lighthouse stands on the rocks just off Robinson's Point, its granite base washed twice each day by the hide tide. A simple white bridge connects the forty-eight-foot tower to the mainland and the keeper's house, which now serves as a bed-and-breakfast inn. Among the few Maine lighthouse built in this century, the light guides fishermen and pleasure boaters passing by Isle au Haut. The beacon flashes red every four seconds.

EAGLE ISLAND LIGHT

Eagle Island, Maine – 1839

For more than a century, an enormous fog bell stood beside the Eagle Island Lighthouse at the top of a sheer, hundred-foot cliff overlooking the eastern passage through Penobscot Bay. In fog and heavy weather, the keeper struck the 1,200-pound brass bell at regular intervals to warn the masters of ships plowing blindly through the passage that dangerous rocks lay nearby. Then the Coast Guard decided to automate and unman the lighthouse. Since there was no longer a keeper to sound the bell, its duties were taken over by buoys out in the channel.

During the summer of 1964, the Coast Guard sent a cutter to the island with a crew of muscular Mainers to remove the big, out-of-work bell. But the massive bell proved more than a match for the burly laborers trying to wrestle it down the hill to the cutter. Something went wrong, and men started shouting. Fortunately for the workers, they all managed to get out of the way as the bell began to roll down toward the cliff. Over it went, banging, clanging, and ringing out like the gongs of hell. When the bell hit the sea, it sent a geyser of water skyward. Then, as the echoes of the bell's clamor died away, members of the crew up on the cliff eyed one another sheepishly and shrugged their shoulders. It is easy to imagine one of them saying: "Well, fellas, we got that rascal down the hill in a wicked hurry and that's for sure."

The Coast Guard workers figured they would leave well enough alone, and for several months the bell lay in the ocean, part of it exposed at each low tide. One day, while working his pots below the Eagle Island cliffs, an enterprising lobsterman named Walter Shepard spotted the bell and got an idea. Shepard hooked a heavy chain to the fallen fog bell and painstakingly towed it several miles through the ocean. Today the salvaged bell is located on Great Spruce Head, outside the family home of noted nature photographer Eliot Porter. There it continues to ring out, serving the Porter family as, perhaps, the world's most impressive dinner bell.

First lit in 1839, during the administration of the nation's eighth president, Martin Van Buren, the Eagle Island Light guides ships over Hardhead Shoals and into Penobscot Bay. One of a chain of lights, including those at Dice Head and Fort Point near the mouth of the Penobscot River, it helped mark a clear path through the rocky bay for a host of nineteenth-century lumber ships. The need for such a well-marked route was clear, since mills were shipping prodigious amounts of lumber down to the sea from Maine's heartland forests. During the mid-1880s shippers loaded more than eight billion board feet of lumber at the inland port of Bangor.

Standing a lofty 106 feet above the water, the light's whitewashed conical tower lifts its lantern just above the treetops on the northeast end of the island. Having changed little since a major renovation in 1858, it continues to guide mariners with its white light, flashing once every four seconds.

HOW TO GET THERE:

The Eagle Island Light can be reached only by water, but to pass this lighthouse by boat is an extraordinary experience. Sailors headed either north or south through the channel between Eagle and Deer islands will see the white tower rise up suddenly, a ghostly giant standing on a forested cliff. Eagle Island is itself a gem, rich in trees, cranberries, and history. To avoid confusion, keep in mind that Maine has several Eagle Islands. The one in Casco Bay, roughly 100 miles to the southwest, was the home of Admiral Robert E. Peary, the first man to reach the North Pole.

DICE HEAD LIGHT

Castine, Maine – 1829 and 1858

Among the oldest and most romantic towns anywhere in North America is Castine, a cluster of old summer cottages and even older sea captains' houses arrayed on a blunt arrow of land pointing directly into Penobscot Bay. Since it guards the entrance to the Penobscot River, seafarers have always coveted this strategic peninsula. As a result, the flags of at least four nations have fluttered above its forts, and the smoke of musket and cannon fire has drifted out across the river many times.

A band of French fur traders established a settlement here in 1614. They were displaced by rival traders from the Plymouth Bay Colony in 1629. The French returned in 1635, but the British Navy drove them out again in 1654. It seemed that nobody could hold the area for long. Dutch pirates overran the town's garrison in 1674. Then came Baron de St. Castine, a wealthy French adventurer who brought peace to the town by marrying the daughter of a troublesome Indian chief named Madockawanda.

By the time the Revolutionary War broke out, the British flag once again flew over the peninsula. In 1779 Paul Revere arrived with an army of Americans who scaled the cliffs along Penobscot Bay and stormed Fort George, standing on the hill above the town. The first assault failed, and Revere's troops never got a chance to regroup and try another. A small British squadron surprised and scattered their supply fleet, sinking nearly forty vessels.

At the start of the War of 1812, the Americans had a fort of their own at Castine, this one named for a president rather than a king. But the defenders of Fort Madison were no match for the huge British fleet that swept down on them early in the war. They fired off a few desultory shots in the general direction of the British ships, spiked their guns, and fled inland as fast as their legs could take them. The British held the town for the balance of the war, billeting their officers and men in private homes and other buildings, many of which still stand.

In 1829 the Lighthouse Service built a tower on Dice Head to help guide lumber ships and other vessels in and out of the Penobscot River. The lighthouse also served to call home the clipper ships of Castine captains on the last leg of trading adventures that often took them as far away as China. Today Castine's harbor is filled with pleasure craft during the summer months, though the clipper ships are gone, along with the crusty sea dogs who sailed them. But young men and women still go down to the sea from Castine. Near the earthen walls of old Fort George is the campus of the Maine Maritime Academy, which offers first-rate degree programs for aspiring merchant seamen.

The Lighthouse Board rebuilt the Dice Head tower in 1858, giving it a six-sided shape and attaching to it an excellent keeper's dwelling. Both the tower and the dwelling are still in good repair, but the lantern has been dark for decades. Its job was long ago taken over by an automated light perched atop a simple skeleton structure down on the rocks beside the bay. The light flashes white every four seconds and can be seen for approximately ten miles.

HOW TO GET THERE:

From U.S. 1, take Route 175 south and then Route 166 or 166A to Castine. Keep your camera handy. This is an outstanding scenic drive, and you may catch a glimpse of the Fort Point Lighthouse, across the bay in Searsport. In Castine, follow Battle Avenue to the lighthouse, which stands on the crest of Dice Head. A public path and wooden stairway lead down to the bay, where a small modern daymark and navigational light is located. While you are gawking at the scenery, a seal may pop its head out of the water to have a look at you.

Be sure to leave time for a tour of this fine old town. Much of the architecture is nineteenth century, and wooden markers tell the stories of the many battles fought here. If you are visiting during the summer, consider having dinner at the Castine Inn, a delightfully unpretentious Down East bed and breakfast. You will want more biscuits. You may also want to buy a copy of the *Castine Patriot*, a straight-talking, small-town New England newspaper. The author of this book was once its editor.

Shown here under siege by dandelions, the old Dice Head Lighthouse has been dark for many years. The people of Castine, one of New England's oldest and most storied villages, maintain the lighthouse and keeper's dwelling, which commands a world-class view of Penobscot Bay.

With its extraordinarily powerful first-order Fresnel lens, the Seguin Island Light ranks among North America's foremost lighthouses. Located on a rocky island several miles off the Maine coast, it is also one of the most isolated. Keepers and their families lived here from 1795, when the station was built, until it was automated during the 1980s.

CHAPTER TWO

Lights of
THE WINTER COAST
WESTERN COAST OF MAINE

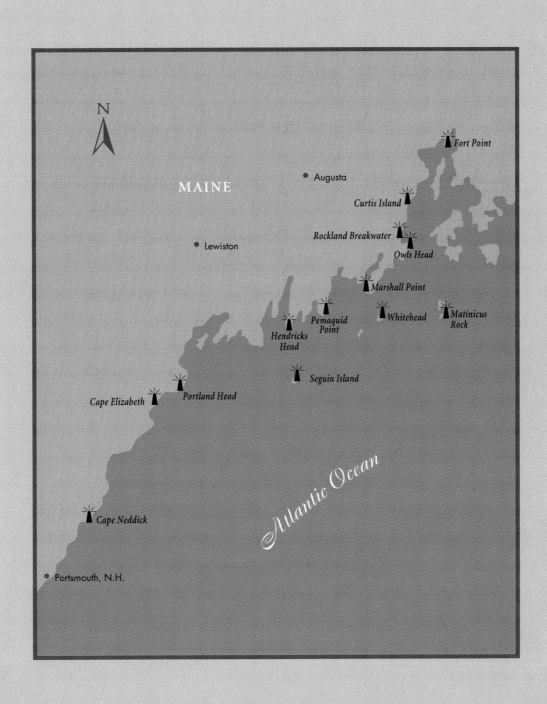

N

MAINE

● Augusta

● Lewiston

Fort Point

Curtis Island

Rockland Breakwater
Owls Head

Marshall Point

Pemaquid
Point
Whitehead

Matinicus
Rock

Hendricks
Head

Seguin Island

Cape Elizabeth   Portland Head

Atlantic Ocean

Cape Neddick

● Portsmouth, N.H.

With its striking white tower and red-roofed dwelling, the Portland Head Lighthouse is a favorite among photographers. Many consider this venerable structure the quintessential lighthouse.

*I*n Maine waters, mariners fear the cold more than the deep. This is especially true in winter, when a shipwrecked sailor is far more likely to freeze to death than to drown. Seamen and fishermen in these parts dread the gales that roll in from the northeast and the blizzards that sweep down out of Canada. These storms often cause temperatures to drop so low that the salt spray from the waves pounding on the side of the ship rattles onto the deck like hail. Ice grips everything, encrusting the hulls and masts of schooners, locking up the clappers of fog bells, and obscuring the windows of lighthouses. Not surprisingly, wrecks are more common in winter than at other times.

The stories of disaster and rescue told by Maine's lighthouse keepers often crackle with ice. They are the sort of tales that should be told only on a summer day or at least beside a warm fire with a hot mug to steady the hand. The following stories have been retold many times and have emptied countless pots of coffee.

THE GHOST SHIP *ISIDORE*

In a graveyard at Kennebunkport is a stone bearing the name of Captain Leander Foss. The body of Captain Foss, however, does not rest anywhere near the stone. It is assumed that Foss went to Davy Jones's locker along with his handsome bark, which disappeared under strange circumstances off Cape Neddick in 1842. But some say that Foss still sails the seas as captain of the ghost ship *Isidore.*

A seaman named Thomas King was supposed to ship out with the *Isidore* when it set sail from Kennebunkport on the last day of November 1842. But two days before the scheduled departure, King woke up in a cold sweat from a terrible dream: a vision of a wrecked ship and drowning sailors. King had no doubt that the vessel in his nightmare was the bark *Isidore* and that the dying men were his fellow crewmen.

King told Foss about his ominous dream, but the old sea captain laughed at him. When Foss refused to delay the *Isidore*'s sailing, King begged to be let out of his contract and left behind. At this point Captain Foss put on a stern face, reminded King that he had already received a month's salary in advance, and told the frightened seaman, in the plainest of language, to be aboard the *Isidore* when it pulled away from the dock.

The following night another member of the *Isidore* crew had a disturbing dream. The sailor saw seven coffins and saw himself in one of them. Foss heard about this second nightmare, but having both little respect for superstition and a schedule to keep, he made up his mind to sail first thing the next morning.

As November 30 dawned the families and friends of the *Isidore*'s crew gathered at the Kennebunkport wharves to wish their loved ones well. But a cloud of dread and gloom hung heavy over the farewell, and there was little of the usual cheering and hat waving as the bark glided slowly out of the harbor. By this time the sky had added a few dark clouds of its own to the scene, and they quickly increased in size and number. It began to snow, and a bitterly cold wind came up out of the north to hurry the *Isidore* rapidly down toward the sea and into the realm of legend.

Among those who watched the *Isidore*'s masts disappear in the snowy distance was Thomas King. He hid in the woods until he was certain that the bark was under way. King expected his acquaintances in town to scorch his ears for having jumped ship, and they did. But his disgrace lasted only about one day.

On the following morning word came to Keenebunkport that pieces of a large ship were scattered all along the shore in the vicinity of Cape Neddick. It was the *Isidore*. There were no survivors of the wreck, and only seven bodies washed ashore—one of them the sailor who had dreamed about the seven coffins. The body of Captain Foss was never found.

Imaginative residents and visitors to Maine's scenic coast have reported many sightings of the *Isidore* during the century and a half since the wreck. They describe a close-reefed bark and shadowy figures who stand motionless on the deck and stare straight ahead. Maybe Thomas King later saw the phantom ship himself—in his dreams if not with his eyes. But if he ever again encountered the ghostly *Isidore,* he never said so.

THE FROZEN LOVERS

A few days before Christmas in the year 1850, a small coasting schooner dropped anchor off Jameson's Point. The vessel was without its captain, who had gone ashore in nearby Rockland and mysteriously disappeared. Some say the captain had been fired; others say he had a premonition and decided to flee from fate. But the schooner's mate, who knew nothing of any dark premonition, saw his master's absence as an opportunity. He had recently proposed to a lovely young woman, and with no one to order him otherwise, he invited her to his cabin.

Only the mate, his bride-to-be, and a deckhand were aboard on the evening of December 22, when a vicious winter gale blew in off the ocean and snapped the schooner's cables. Although the sailors fought hard to save their vessel, the storm drove it relentlessly forward, finally crushing its hull on the cruel ledges near Owls Head. Held in a viselike grip by the rocks, the schooner filled with seawater but did not sink. Instead, it became a target for giant waves, which threw spouts of freezing spray over the three frightened people huddled on its deck. Their clothes and even their skin quickly became rough and crusty with ice.

The mate knew that he and his fellow shipwreck victims would soon freeze to death unless something was done. Faced with the horror of having coaxed his beloved into an apparent death trap, he came up with a desperate plan. To save themselves, he and his companions would roll up in a blanket and lie down together beside the stern rail. The mate hoped the freezing spray would form a protective shell of ice on the outside of the blanket. This it did, but the ice grew much thicker than he had anticipated. All night the sea continued to douse the three until they were entombed in a layer of ice several inches thick.

Under the suffocating weight of the ice, the mate and his girl lost consciousness, and by morning the deckhand believed that he was the only one left alive. Slashing at the ice with a small knife and using his bleeding hands as hammers, he managed to free himself. When he was strong enough to stand, the sailor saw that the tide had gone out and a narrow bridge of exposed rock now connected the schooner with the shore. So, bloodied and nearly frozen, he dropped down off the deck and stumbled off toward the Owls Head Light, which he could see shining through the storm. Overwhelmed by cold and exhaustion, he made the last part of the journey crawling on his hands and knees. But he eventually reached his destination, and in the warm kitchen of the keeper's dwelling, he told his incredible story.

The keeper had little hope of finding anyone alive aboard the schooner; nevertheless, he organized a rescue party and headed for the wreck. There the rescuers found a man and a woman locked in a lover's embrace and frozen in a solid block of ice. It took picks, chisels, knives, and several strong men to free the pair. Everyone was sure they were dead; even so, an attempt was made to revive them. Hurried ashore to a home near the lighthouse, their seemingly lifeless bodies were treated with cold-water baths and constant massage. In two hours the woman regained consciousness. An hour after that the mate also showed signs of life. It took the two several months to recover from their ordeal, but by June they were strong enough to stand together in front of a preacher and pronounce their vows.

Ironically, the sailor whose grueling trek through the storm had brought help and saved the lovers from certain death never fully recovered from his adventure. He did not go to sea again and lived out his life on waterfronts of towns near Owls Head. He never tired of telling strangers about his struggle in the blizzard of 1850 and about the frozen lovers of Owls Head.

FORT POINT LIGHT

Searsport, Maine – 1836

During the mid-nineteenth century as many as 200 lumber ships might pass the square-towered Fort Point Light in a single week. All of them were on their way to or from the bustling inland port of Bangor, abut twenty-five miles up the Penobscot River.

Built in 1836 by order of President Andrew Jackson, the lighthouse, along with the lights at Eagle Island and Dice Head, pointed the way into the mouth of the river and beyond to the world's busiest lumber port. Over the years billions of board feet of lumber, cut from Maine's tall forests, moved down the river past the light. The wood was used to build homes, businesses, bridges, and fences in Boston and other cities along the U.S. East Coast.

Although not much taller than the attached keeper's dwelling, the tower stands on a high promontory, its light eighty-eight feet above the water. The lantern still contains the same Fresnel prism lens installed when the Lighthouse Board decided to renovate the station in 1857. It displays a fixed white light. The fog-bell house still stands and is one of the last of its kind.

Near the lighthouse are the ruins of Fort Pownall, a key military outpost established in 1759 during the French and Indian War. British and American armies fought two battles here during the Revolutionary War.

HOW TO GET THERE:

Turn off U.S. 1 toward Penobscot Bay at Stockton Springs and follow signs to Fort Point State Park and the Fort Pownall Memorial. Occupied by a state park employee, the keeper's dwelling is closed to the public. The lighthouse grounds offer a sweeping view of the bay.

Fort Point Lighthouse is reflected in a window of the building housing the station fog bell. The building is listed in the National Register of Historic Places; the fog bell is a rare survivor of the old lighthouse establishment.

MATINICUS ROCK LIGHT

South of Matinicus Island, Maine – 1827, 1846, and 1857

Located about twenty-five miles from Rockland, the nearest mainland port, Matinicus Rock is truly a remote outpost. Fog blankets the treeless island one out of every five days. When there is no fog, wind tears at the rock, and storms blast it with such fury that giant boulders are shifted by the surf. Exposed to the very worst that the sea can throw at it, this would seem an unlikely place to build a lighthouse with wood. But that is exactly what the Lighthouse Service did, throwing up two relatively flimsy wooden towers on the island in 1827.

John Shaw, the station's first keeper, must have shaken his head in dismay at the sight of the white, wood-frame towers. They would surely fall in the first muscular nor'easter. But, surprisingly, the towers stood up to the sea's anger a lot longer than did Shaw. Sixty-five years old when he took over the new station, Shaw fell desperately ill during his third year as keeper. By early the next year, the old man was dead, the life drummed out of him by the sea and the rock.

Although most of them were much younger than Shaw, few of the keepers who followed him lasted very long on the rock. During its first decade the station killed or drove off its keepers at an average of one every two years.

The wooden towers themselves endured for just under twenty years, but by 1846 they were totally ramshackle and had to be replaced. This time the builders used granite. Ironically, the new stone towers lasted only half as long as the wooden towers before them. In 1857 the Lighthouse Board pulled them down and erected the taller cut-granite towers that still stand on the island today. Only one of the towers remains in use, however; its white light flashes once every ten seconds.

Surely the rock's most remarkable resident was its heroine, Abbie Burgess. She was only seventeen when a stubborn gale blew up out of the Atlantic in 1856 and cut the station off from the mainland for nearly four weeks. When the storm hit, keeper Samuel Burgess was in Rockland buying supplies for his family and medicine for his bedridden wife. He had left his daughter Abbie to look after his wife and three younger daughters. Also, having taught Abbie to trim the fourteen lamps in each of the two towers, he counted on her to keep the all-important Matinicus Rock lights burning.

The storm struck suddenly, packing winds so strong that boats could make no headway against them. Trapped in Rockland, Burgess could do nothing to help his family. As days stretched into weeks, with no break in the relentless gale, the keeper despaired. But sea captains who had fought their way out of the storm into the safety of Rockland's calm harbor brought hope. Those who had passed close to Matinicus Rock reported that they had seen lights in the towers.

After nearly a month the winds finally let up, and Burgess was able to sail back home. What he found there astonished him. The storm had destroyed much of the light station. Only the foundation of the keeper's dwelling remained; the rest had been washed into the sea. But thanks to Abbie, the Burgess family had survived. As the first dark clouds bore down on the rock, she had moved her mother and sisters out of the dwelling and into one of the stone towers. There she had cared for them and kept their spirits high, and never once in four weeks had she let the lights fail.

Abbie eventually married the son of a lighthouse keeper, and together they kept the twin lights of Matinicus Rock. She had four children, all of them born on the rock. Abbie Burgess Grant is buried in Forest Hills Cemetery, on Spruce Head Island. Her gravestone is a replica of her lighthouse.

The classical Fresnel lens that once shined on Matinicus Rock is now on display at the Shore Village Museum in Rockland, Maine. This is one of the best and most complete lighthouse museums in the country. For information or directions to Abbie's grave, call (207) 594–0311.

HOW TO GET THERE:

Special arrangements can sometimes be made with some boating companies for trips to the island. Visits usually require an overnight stay on rustic Matinicus Island, about 6 miles north of the rock. For ferry information, call (207) 366–3700. During the spring and summer months, a large colony of colorful puffins nests on the rock. Access to the island is restricted, especially during puffin mating season. The trip is well worth the time, since seven or eight lighthouses can be viewed from the boat, and finback whale sightings are not unusual.

Located about twenty-five miles out in the Atlantic, Matinicus Rock Lighthouse was among the most isolated, challenging, and dangerous duty stations for keepers. Now automated, the station is home to a large colony of puffins.

CURTIS ISLAND LIGHT

Camden, Maine – 1836

Pleasure sailors and schooner captains who see the fixed green light on Curtis Island know that the charming town of Camden and its well-maintained harbor lie just beyond. Camden, with its scenic mountains and ocean vistas, is one of the most popular tourist centers along the Maine coast.

Camden was once a busy port and home to dozens of merchant-ship captains who roamed the world in search of a profit. For many of these sea traders, the light shining from atop the Curtis Island tower, fifty-two feet above the water, was a welcome sight. It offered them their first glimpse of home, often after an absence of several years.

Curtis Island is named for Cyrus Curtis, a Mainer who became world famous and fabulously wealthy as a publisher of family magazines such as the *Saturday Evening Post.* Long ago, however, it was known as Negro Island, for the black sailor, who according to legend, once lived alone there in Robinson Crusoe fashion.

HOW TO GET THERE:

Since it is located on the south (seaward) side of the island, the light is difficult to see from land. A view can be had, however, by turning toward the water at the Camden Post Office and following Penobscot Avenue. The lighthouse will appear on the left as you approach the end of the road. For more precise directions and suggestions on how to see the light, ask at the visitors' center beside Camden Harbor.

Several schooners, such as the Stephen Tabor *and the* Roseway, *operate out of the harbor during warm-weather months. They offer sailing tours of a week or more in length. The most charming way to see Curtis Island Light may be from the deck of one of these wonderful old vessels.*

ROCKLAND BREAKWATER LIGHT

Rockland, Maine – 1888 and 1902

During the nineteenth century Maine began to produce and ship prodigious quantities of lime to markets all over America. Much of this lime, used by construction crews for making mortar and cement, passed through the mid-coast port of Rockland. Because Rockland had a relatively unprotected harbor, lime freighters lying at anchor there were endangered by waves rolling in from the broad Penobscot Bay.

To correct this problem and make the harbor safe, the town decided to build a long stone breakwater, extending nearly a mile from Jameson's Point out into the bay. But no sooner had construction begun than the breakwater itself became a significant navigational obstacle. On foggy days especially, near misses by ships sailing in and out of the harbor were common. So, workers erected a light, moving it a little farther seaward with the completion of each new section of breakwater. This "traveling" lighthouse served effectively as a temporary measure. Then, when the Rockland Breakwater was completed in 1888, the Lighthouse Service established a permanent light station at the far end.

Rebuilt along with the breakwater in 1902, the station consists of a white, square tower and an attached two-story keeper's dwelling. The station has a powerful foghorn, and its lens, located thirty-nine feet above the water, throws out a bright white flash every five seconds.

Built in 1902, Rockland Breakwater Light marks the end of a mile-long stone jetty.

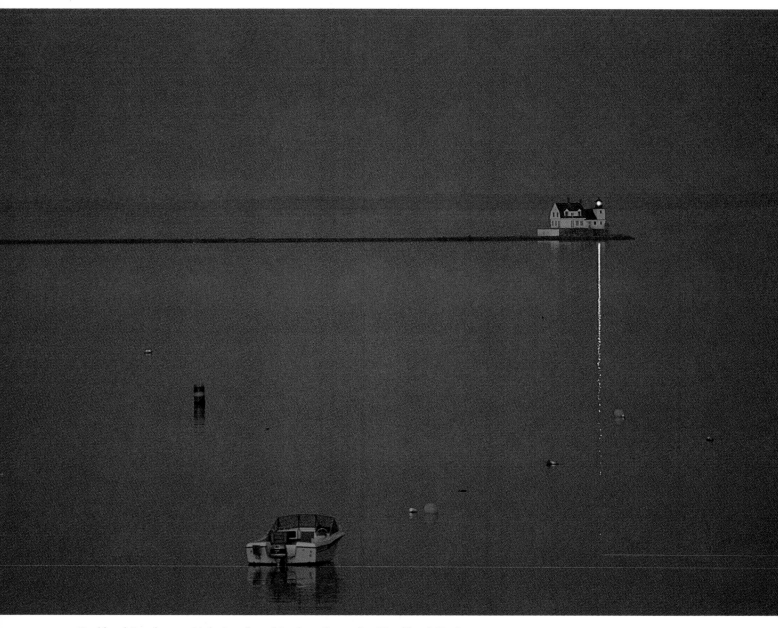

Rockland Breakwater Light is reflected in the soft purple of Rockland Harbor at sunset.

HOW TO GET THERE:

From U.S. 1, turn toward the water onto Waldo Avenue, just north of downtown Rockland. Then turn right onto Samoset Road. Samoset Road is only about ½ mile long, and when you reach its end, the breakwater will be just ahead and on your right. You can also get an excellent view of the lighthouse from the decks of the car ferries that serve North Haven (207–867–4441), Vinalhaven (207–863–4421), and Bass Harbor (207–244–3254) islands .

While in Rockland, be sure to stop at 104 Limerock Street and see the Shore Village Museum, generally regarded as having the most comprehensive display of lighthouse materials in the New England area. The array of magnificent Fresnel lenses includes the second-order lens from Minots Ledge and the classic fourth-order lens from Baker's Island Lighthouse. Hear the deep moan of foghorns and feel the weight of the old fog bell, once rung for exhaustive hours in warning. For more information, call (207) 594–0311.

OWLS HEAD LIGHT

Rockland, Maine – 1826

ailors headed for Rockland sometimes swear that they can see the face of a giant bird sculpted by nature into the rocks of the promontory southeast of the town. They point at two caves forming the eyes and rocky outcroppings giving the great bird a nose and beak as well as a pair of owlish ears. "There it is," they say. "Can't you see it?" Others laugh and say that they see nothing on Owls Head but rocks—and a Coast Guard light station.

Built during the presidency of John Quincy Adams to guide lime freighters into Rockland Harbor, the lighthouse is one of the oldest in New England. Unlike most other old light stations, its tower has never been pulled down and rebuilt. The tower is only about twenty feet tall, but because it rises from a high promontory, its fixed white light shines from about one hundred feet above the water. A fifth-order Fresnel lens focuses the light, which can be seen from about sixteen miles at sea.

The mysterious owl in Owls Head has seen many strange happenings. Consider, for instance, the saga of the frozen lovers described in the introduction to this chapter (see page 36).

In 1745 a party of Indians on Owls Head captured Thomas Sanders, a young English sailor. But Sanders proved a bit too quick for his captors. He asked them to loan him a musket so that he could "shoot some ducks." In a truly extraordinary display of gullibility, the Indians obliged, and Sanders, brandishing the borrowed musket, escaped into the woods.

In the early summer of 1757, a fleet of thirty canoes brought a large Penobscot Indian war party to Owls Head. A small force of white soldiers fought off the attackers and, turning the tables on the Indians, scalped two of them.

As they sailed out of Rockland Harbor on November 9, 1844, sailors on the fine new brig *Maine* may have looked back at Owls Head and argued over whether or not, indeed, it resembled the head of an owl. None of them would ever get another chance to resolve the question. This was the *Maine*'s maiden voyage—and also its last voyage.

Its tower only about twenty feet tall, Owls Head is Maine's stubbiest lighthouse. Legends concerning it abound, however, and in this sense, the little lighthouse can be said to be many-storied.

Mariners swore that they could see the head and tufted ears of a great stone owl on this point. Since 1826 Owls Head Light has helped keep ships away from the dangerous rocks here.

The *Maine* never arrived in New Orleans, where it was scheduled to deliver a load of Rockland lime. As if plucked from the seas by a giant predatory bird, the brig disappeared, along with its crew of nine. Then, three years later, a ship dropped anchor in Rockland Harbor. On board were a mahogany chest, a ship's atlas, and a navigation book, which local people swore belonged to members of the *Maine*'s crew. According to the captain of the visiting vessel, three Portuguese sailors had left these items behind when they jumped ship in Vera Cruz. No further traces were ever found of the *Maine* or her crew.

During the 1930s Owls Head Light had, believe it or not, a dog as an assistant keeper. The dog, a sharp-eared springer spaniel named Spot, barked loudly whenever he heard a ship. He would also ring the fog bell by pulling on the rope with his teeth. It is said that Spot once saved the Matinicus mail boat from smashing into the Owls Head rocks. A blizzard had cut visibility to near zero and frozen up the fog bell so that it could not be rung. But mail-boat Captain Stuart Ames heard the alert dog's persistent barking and managed to bear off from the rocks in time to avert disaster.

HOW TO GET THERE:

From U.S. 1 in Rockland, take Route 73 south for about 2 miles. Turn left, drive 2½ miles, and, a few hundred yards past the Owls Head Post Office, turn left again onto Lighthouse Road. After less than a mile, you will reach a barrier and a small dirt parking lot. You cannot see the lighthouse from the parking lot, but don't be discouraged. Walk around the barrier and continue on foot. Just ahead is one of the grandest views and most charming lighthouses you are ever likely to enjoy. But take care, especially with children, since the cliffs on either side of the road are steep.

WHITEHEAD LIGHT

Off Tenants Harbor, Maine – 1807 and 1852

uilt by order of President Thomas Jefferson in 1807, Whitehead is one of the oldest lighthouse stations in Maine. It also produced one of the earliest Lighthouse Service scandals, when the station's very first keeper, Ellis Dolph, perhaps dissatisfied with his low government salary, decided to make a little money on the side. The scandal surfaced when officials noticed that the Whitehead lamps seemed to have an insatiable appetite for whale oil. An inspector sent up from Boston to investigate discovered that the lamps were not the problem. He found citizens all over Thomaston and Rockland who had purchased oil from Dolph. These people had been told that the oil came from a surplus supply belonging to the keeper, but this was not the case. Instead, Dolph dipped it right out of the government tank beside the lighthouse tower at Whitehead. Dolph was fired but apparently was not prosecuted for his "double dipping."

Rebuilt by the Lighthouse Board in 1852, the station now consists of a square granite tower, rising approximately seventy-five feet above the water, and an attached red-brick service building. It guides mariners with a green light that occults once every four seconds.

Sailors often count themselves lucky to see the Whitehead Light at all. This stretch of the Maine coast is one of the foggiest places in North America. The light station is socked in by fog an average of once every five days for a total of nearly 2,000 hours per year. For this reason, an effective fog bell was always considered indispensable here. In fact, the bell was in such constant use that keepers rigged up a mechanical device to ring it automatically. This contraption was powered by the waves and tides and struck the 2,000-pound bell four times each minute with a fifteen-pound hammer. The constant ringing must have given the keepers some terrible headaches.

HOW TO GET THERE:

The lighthouse cannot be reached by land and is most easily viewed from the air or water. The third-order Fresnel lens from the tower is now on display at the Shore Village Museum in Rockland, Maine. More accessible is the Marshall Point Light, just outside Port Clyde, a charming fishing village. From U.S. 1 at Thomaston, take Route 131 through St. George and Tenants Harbor to Port Clyde. Erected in 1832 and rebuilt in 1858, the tower is about 30 feet tall and is connected to land by a bridge. It displays a fixed white light.

A shrouded sentinel, Whitehead Lighthouse stands on one of the foggiest stretches of coast in North America. Its foghorn was once powered by the tides.

PEMAQUID POINT LIGHT

Pemaquid Point, Maine – 1827 and 1857

Old sailors enjoy pointing out that "the fog itself is not a problem; it's what you can't see because of the fog that gets you into trouble—like ships or shoals." Or big storms.

On the afternoon of September 16, 1903, the fishing schooner *George Edmunds* was plowing through a thick fog several miles off the Maine coast. Suddenly, like a curtain rolling up at the start of a drama, the fog lifted. Captain

Willard Poole could see now, and he was glad enough of that. But he did not like what he saw. The fog had hidden from him a bank of angry black clouds, and the storm was now bearing down on the *Edmunds*. Alarmed, the captain gave the order to make for land.

Poole could see the flash of Pemaquid Point Light and steered directly for it. He knew that the calm waters of St. John's Bay lay just beyond the light. But the *Edmunds*

Ocean waves have carved images of themselves on these unique formations. Shown here catching the last rays of sunlight on a summer day, the Pemaquid Point Lighthouse warns mariners not to sail onto these rocks.

would never reach the bay. Sailors familiar with the area knew that a course for St. John's Bay must be "shaped" so as to avoid a point of land just west of the lighthouse. Poole tried to do this but misjudged his course by about 1,000 feet. The *Edmunds* struck hard on the rocks and was quickly dashed to fragments by the stormy sea. The captain drowned, and only two of his thirteen crew members survived the disaster.

Thanks to the lighthouse, active since 1827, only a few such wrecks have occurred off Pemaquid. The original lighthouse was built during the presidency of John Quincy Adams for $4,000. The Lighthouse Board saw fit to rebuilt the tower in 1857 and fit it with a fourth-order Fresnel lens. The rubblestone tower is only thirty-eight feet tall, but since it sits on a high cliff, the light flashes out over the sea from a point seventy-nine feet above the water.

HOW TO GET THERE:

Turn south off U.S. 1 at Damariscotta and follow Route 130 for approximately 16 miles to the Pemaquid Point parking lot. Sculpted by nature, the extraordinary rock formations here remind some of water thrown up by the pounding surf and about to run back into the sea. At the lighthouse, the keeper's dwelling now houses the fascinating Fishermen's Museum. For more information, call the museum at (207) 677–2494. The museum is open by appointment in winter; call (207) 677–2726.

The whitewashed picket fence and lovely old stone tower of Pemaquid Point Lighthouse stand in stark contrast to the deep blue of the sky and ocean. One of the more scenic spots along the entire U.S. East Coast, the point is a magnet for tourists and picnickers.

HENDRICKS HEAD LIGHT

Boothbay Harbor, Maine – 1829 and 1875

One March not long after the Civil War, a late-winter blizzard blasted the coast of Maine. The storm wrecked many ships. One of them, a hapless schooner, struck a shoal not half a mile from the Hendricks Head Lighthouse.

The frantic keeper found that he could not launch the station's rescue dory in the pounding surf. Unable to assist the schooner's desperate crew, he was forced to stand by helplessly while the shipwrecked sailors froze to death in the ship's rigging. The keeper did build a bonfire to give the sailors the comfort of knowing that they had at least been seen. He could do nothing else.

The disconsolate keeper was sure that all aboard had perished. Then he spotted what he later described as a "curious bundle tossing lightly in the thundering sea." The keeper and his wife managed to pull the bundle, a feather mattress, out of the surf. To their amazement, they heard cries coming from within the ice-encrusted mattress. Chipping away at the ice and ripping open the mattress, they discovered a small sea chest and, inside that, a baby— frightened but very much alive. Accompanying the child was a note from the schooner's captain and his wife explaining that they had "committed [their daughter] into God's hands." The disaster hadn't been total after all.

Commissioned in 1829, the Hendricks Head Lighthouse stands on a rocky point on Southport Island, overlooking the mouth of the Sheepscot River. The light helped guide fishing boats into Boothbay Harbor and freighters along a dangerous stretch of coast south of the powerful Seguin Island Lighthouse.

In 1875 the original structure was replaced by a forty-foot brick tower and a separate, wooden keeper's dwelling. A bell tower was added in 1890. The government decommissioned the light in 1933 during the Great Depression and eventually sold the land to private interests. The old lighthouse has been restored to near-perfect condition by the current owners, who use it as a year-round residence.

The square brick tower and detached wooden dwelling shown in this contemporary view of Hendricks Head Lighthouse replaced the orginal lighthouse in 1875. (Courtesy of Ben Russell)

HOW TO GET THERE:

From U.S. Highway 1, turn toward the ocean on Route 27 and follow it for 10 miles to Lakeside Drive. Turn right onto Lakeside and, after about 2½ miles, turn right again and cross a bridge onto Southport Island. The lighthouse is located on Beach Road, approximately 3 miles straight ahead. The lighthouse is on private property, so please respect the rights of the owners. Nearby are Boothbay and Boothbay Harbor, both well known for their seafood and as haunts for droves of summer visitors.

SEGUIN ISLAND LIGHT

Seguin Island, Maine – 1795 and 1819

With its lantern located 186 feet above the sea and fitted with a powerful first-order Fresnel lens, the Seguin Island Light ranks as one of America's foremost lighthouses. On clear evenings its fixed white light has been seen some forty miles out at sea. One of the nation's oldest light stations, it has the only first-order lens still operational in Maine. George Washington himself gave the order to build the first tower here in 1795, and Congress appropriated $6,300 to see the job done right.

But despite the money allocated, which was considerable for the time, the tower was constructed of wood. By 1819 the sea had completely dilapidated the lighthouse, and it had to be rebuilt. This time the builders used stone and billed the government less than $2,500.

The original wooden tower lasted less than twenty-five years, but it stood up to Seguin's harsh weather a lot longer than did Count John Polersky, the station's first keeper. Born to a noble family in Alsace, Polersky immigrated to America, where he served as a major in Washington's Continental Army. Polersky's salary was set at $200 per year, not a handsome income for a European nobleman nor even for a Revolutionary War officer. Polersky pleaded for a raise but was repeatedly turned down. Meanwhile, the station's cruel weather turned his home into a shack, smashed and sank his three boats, tore apart his barns, beat down his gardens, and left his health in ruins. After five years on the island, during which time he faithfully tended the light, Polersky died.

Located in the mouth of the Kennebec River, the Seguin Light station stands on historic ground. Two small ships, the *Gift of God* and the *Mary and John*, dropped anchor near the island in 1607. They had brought settlers

The Friends of Seguin Island, a nonprofit corporation, now maintains and preserves the lighthouse. There are monthly boat trips from the Maine Maritime Museum, in Bath, during the summer. For current information, write to Friends of Seguin Island, Box 438, Georgetown, ME 04548.

who hoped to establish the first English colony in North America. The settlers planted a flag and built a small town on the banks of the Kennebec. But hunger, hardship, and a terrible Maine winter killed many and caused the survivors to abandon the colony and sail back home to England. No doubt the would-be colonists wished they had never seen Seguin Island.

Even the Indians, who gave Seguin its name, were wary of the island. Seguin is an English corruption of an Indian word loosely translated as "place where the sea vomits." Considering that Indian fishermen had to fight the choppy seas at the mouth of the Kennebec in flimsy canoes, they may have intended to describe Seguin as the place where they themselves vomited.

The Pond Island (top left) and Perkins Island (right) lighthouses stand above stone ramparts guarding the banks of Maine's legendary Kennebec River. Navy destroyers built upriver at the Bath Iron Works make their maiden voyage down to the sea through this channel. The small, white structure (left), actually a tiny lighthouse, helps mark the safe passage.

HOW TO GET THERE:

Located on an island about 2 miles from Popham Beach at the mouth of the Kennebec River, the lighthouse cannot be reached by land. But the tower and light can be viewed at a distance from Popham Beach. Turn onto Route 209 off U.S. 1 at Bath. During the summer tour boats from Boothbay Harbor offer views of the light. The Maine Maritime Museum, in Bath, runs tour boats (207–443–1316) to the island throughout the summer. For independent boat tours, call (207) 389–1883. A magnificent view is offered from the rocky bluffs and tower. An excellent small museum (207–371–2508) depicts the history of the island and its keepers through vintage photographs and maritime artifacts.

By taking short side roads off Route 209 along the way to Popham Beach, you can also see Perkins Island Light and Squirrel Point Light. Both built in 1898, these lighthouses mark the Kennebec River channel.

PORTLAND HEAD LIGHT

South Portland, Maine – 1791

The nation's first Congress under the Constitution convened in New York City in 1789. Its initial order of business was the Bill of Rights, but the ink was barely dry on that honorable document before Congress turned its attention to lighthouses. President George Washington had a particular interest in ocean and river commerce and wanted all lighthouses and other navigational aids brought under the wing of the new federal government. On August 7, 1789, Congress obliged the president by passing one of the earliest federal laws, an act setting up a "Lighthouse Establishment"—or, as it would later be known, the Lighthouse Service.

Under provisions of the act, the government took over ownership and responsibility for eleven lighthouses along the nation's Atlantic shores, including the famed Boston Light, built in 1716. The list would have numbered an even dozen except that construction of the important Portland Head Light, begun two years earlier by the Commonwealth of Massachusetts, was still far from complete. Massachusetts had fallen on hard financial times and could no longer afford to pay for the project. An impatient Washington told Secretary of the Treasury Alexander Hamilton to get the project moving. Hamilton squeezed $1,500 out of Congress, only enough money to build a tower with fieldstone dragged to the construction site by oxen, but by late in 1790, the tower stood ready, its lantern nearly one hundred feet above the water. The builders did their job well. The tower has survived almost 200 years of pounding by the

Perhaps the most visited and photographed lighthouse in New England, Portland Head Light has shone from countless posters, calendars, bank checks, and postcards.

persistent Atlantic. On January 10, 1891, keeper Joseph Greenleaf put a match to the station's lamps, and the lantern where he stood has rarely been darkened since.

Driven for more than a century by a second-order Fresnel lens (now replaced by a rotating, airport-style beacon), the flashing light on Portland Head has guided countless vessels to safe harbor. One that never made it, however, was the steamer *Bohemian*. Bound from Liverpool, England, to the United States with 218 passengers, many of them immigrants, the *Bohemian* was just short of its goal when it met with disaster on February 22, 1868. Plowing through heavy seas and fog toward Portland, the steamer slammed into Alden's Rock, a few miles south of the lighthouse. The rock tore through the *Bohemian*'s tough iron hull as if through thin wooden planking, and people were soon

jumping into lifeboats. The fully loaded Number Two boat broke away from its hoist and dropped, dumping several dozen people into the winter sea. Most of them quickly froze to death or drowned. Five other lifeboats reached shore safely, however, and riding in one of them was an Irish boy named John Fitzgerald. Boston would later know Fitzgerald as an astute politician.

Another wreck, some twenty years after the *Bohemian* disaster, brought the three-masted bark *Annie Maguire* right into the front yard of Portland Head Light's keeper Joshua Strout. Ironically, the *Maguire* was in deep financial and legal trouble, and creditors planned to lay claim to the ship the moment that it dropped anchor in Portland Harbor. The sheriff had asked Strout to be on the lookout for the vessel and notify authorities as soon as it sailed into sight.

Stout's task proved much easier than he expected. On Christmas Eve 1888 the bark appeared suddenly out of a storm and ran up onto the rocks only a few yards from Strout's front door on Portland Head. Drawn away from their Christmas tree by the collision, which sounded to them like an earthquake, the Strout family ran outside and pitched in to rescue the *Maguire*'s fifteen-man crew. Later the sheriff was able to serve papers on the beleaguered ship right there at the lighthouse, but this accomplished little for the new owners. The *Maguire* was so beaten up by the wreck that she later sold at auction for only $177.

Portland Head Light was automated on August 7, 1989, during Lighthouse Service Bicentennial celebration. The keeper's dwelling was given to the town of Cape Elizabeth.

HOW TO GET THERE:

One of the most visited and most often photographed lighthouses in North America, the Portland Head Light stands adjacent to Fort Williams State Park, near South Portland. From U.S. 1, take Highway 1A, Route 77, and Shore Road. Turn left into Fort Williams Park and follow signs to the lighthouse parking lot. The Portland Head Museum is open weekdays January through October, 10:00 A.M. to 4:00 P.M., and on weekends until December 20. For current information, call the museum at (207) 799–2661.

Workmen prepare to lower part of the light apparatus as the Portland Head Lighthouse is automated in 1989.

CAPE ELIZABETH LIGHT

Cape Elizabeth, Maine – 1828 and 1874

Like Matinicus Rock, farther up the Maine coast, Cape Elizabeth once guided mariners with a pair of lights. In fact, the station was for many years known as "Two Lights." The two Cape Elizabeth towers, spaced about 300 yards apart, displayed a fixed light and a flashing light, respectively. When approaching the coast from the east, south, or west, a ship's position could be found quickly on a chart once a sailor had spotted the double

The Cape Elizabeth Lighthouse has a distinctively nautical appearance. The keeper's home is now privately owned.

lights. But today only one light shines on the cape. In 1924 officials decided the second light was redundant and discontinued it.

The station has a long history. A forty-five-foot octagonal tower was erected on Cape Elizabeth in 1811 as a daymark, but it was of no use at all to ships' captains blinded by fog or darkness. So, under pressure from shipping interests, the government paid contractor Jeremiah Berry $4,250 to replace the daymark with two rubblestone towers. Working fast, Berry had both towers ready for service in less than five months, and their lamps were first lit in October 1828.

By 1874 both lighthouses had been all but destroyed by the weather and the sea, so they were pulled down, and a pair of handsome cast-iron towers was erected in their place. When the west light was discontinued in 1924, the lantern was removed from the tower. But the east tower still looks much the way it did more than a century ago. Standing on a high cliff and with a second-order Fresnel lens throwing out bursts of six rapid flashes every thirty seconds, it ranks as one of the most powerful lights in New England. Astoundingly, sailors can see the Cape Elizabeth Light from up to twenty-seven miles away.

Despite the power and effectiveness of the light, the rocky cape has continued over the years to claim ships. The schooner *Australia* struck rocks near the lighthouse during a blizzard on January 28, 1885. The keeper rescued two members of its crew. In addition to the *Austrailia*, the 286-ton bark *Tasmania,* the schooner *Abigail,* the schooner *Susan,* and many other ships were lost within sight of the station and its keepers.

On March 3, 1947, the coal freighter *Oakley L. Alexander* ran head-on into a storm so violent that the ship was broken in half. All thirty-two members of the ship's crew managed to clamber aboard the stern section, which continued to float. The accident took place more than eight miles from shore, but, luckily for the crew, the wind was blowing toward land. The stern ended up on the rocks near the Cape Elizabeth Lighthouse. Using a lifesaving device called a Lyle gun, coastguardsman Earle Drinkwater fired a line over the stern and started hauling men ashore. Eventually, he was able to save the entire crew.

HOW TO GET THERE:

The Portland Head and Cape Elizabeth lights can be visited in a single afternoon. From Portland Head, return to Route 77 and turn left. Turn left again onto Ocean House Road and enter Two Lights State Park, where signs will lead you to the lighthouse. Or, from U.S. 1A in South Portland, turn south onto Route 77 and follow it to Ocean House Road. Take your camera. The keeper's house at Cape Elizabeth is private property, but there are good viewing areas nearby.

The Spring Point Lighthouse marks the end of a long breakwater near Portland, Maine. For rather obvious reasons, this type of lighthouse is referred to as a "sparkplug." Built atop heavy, concrete-filled caissons and armored with iron plates, sparkplug lighthouses are designed to withstand high waves and heavy weather in open water.

CAPE NEDDICK LIGHT

York, Maine – 1879

Just off Cape Neddick, near the old town of York, Maine, lies a small barren island long known to fisherman as the "Nubble." Here the rocks seem to have boiled up out of the sea, and nature has created a sculpture garden by carving fantastic shapes into the exposed stone. Below the century-old lighthouse is a rock formation called the Devil's Oven. As if to warn the devil against cooking up anything too evil in his oven, a stone preacher's pulpit stands nearby. But the most famous formation on the Nubble is Washington's Rock. Visitors often say they can see a striking likeness of the nation's first president in the rock—but most agree that it takes some imagination.

Earlier visitors may have seen other faces in the stones of the Nubble. Perhaps Captain Bartholomew Gosnold, the English explorer who anchored beside the Nubble in 1602, saw the face of an Indian chief in the rock. Gosnold met here with coastal natives and later named the place Savage Rock. Following the mysterious destruction of the *Isidore* (see page 36), local folk may have seen the faces of phantom sailors in the Nubble's stones.

Probably no one has ever noticed a likeness of President Rutherford B.Hayes in the rocks of the island, but it was he who signed the order establishing a light station here in 1879. The government spent $15,000 building the lighthouse, keeper's dwelling, and support buildings.

The tower, though only forty feet tall, stands on the island's highest point; consequently, its light shines from an elevation of eighty-eight feet. The light flashes red every six seconds.

At least three weddings have been held at the Cape Neddick Lighthouse. One of these ceremonies was performed in the lantern room itself.

HOW TO GET THERE:

From U.S. 1 in York, take Route 1A to York Beach, turn right onto Nubble Road, and proceed about 1 mile onto Nubble Point. You can enjoy an excellent view of the lighthouse from the point, but do not attempt to cross over onto Nubble Island—the footing is dangerous and the tides may strand you on the island.

With sunlight still glinting from the upstairs windows of the keeper's house, the "Nubble" Lighthouse on Cape Neddick projects its first red flash of the night.

Sweeping in from the open Atlantic, a threatening bank of clouds sets a somber mood at Highland (also known as Cape Cod) Lighthouse.

CHAPTER THREE

Lights of
FREEDOM'S SHORES

NEW HAMPSHIRE and MASSACHUSETTS

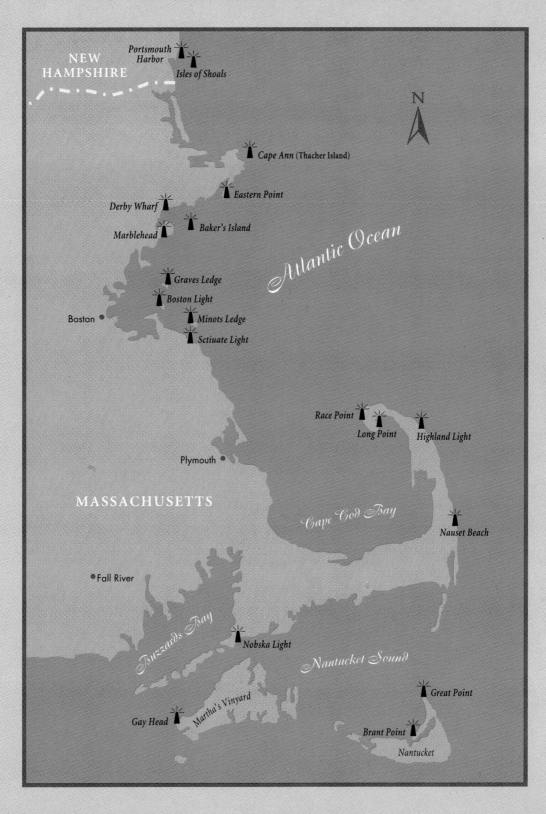

NEW HAMPSHIRE

Portsmouth Harbor

Isles of Shoals

N

Cape Ann (Thacher Island)

Eastern Point

Derby Wharf

Baker's Island

Marblehead

Atlantic Ocean

Graves Ledge

Boston Light

Boston

Minots Ledge

Sctiuate Light

Race Point

Long Point

Highland Light

Plymouth

MASSACHUSETTS

Cape Cod Bay

Nauset Beach

Fall River

Buzzards Bay

Nobska Light

Nantucket Sound

Great Point

Gay Head

Martha's Vinyard

Brant Point

Nantucket

Among the last of a hardy breed, U.S. coastguardsman Dennis Devers looks out toward the Atlantic from the grounds of Boston Light Station, where he served for several years as full-time keeper. Computers and automatic relays have taken over the work of keepers, and lighthouses throughout North America now stand their vigils alone.

On the night of April 18, 1775, Paul Revere watched for a signal from a makeshift lighthouse—the steeple of Boston's Old North Church. Soon a fellow patriot would raise a lantern in the steeple and send Revere riding hell-bent for Concord and Lexington and shouting his famous message: "The British are coming!" It is easy to imagine that, while he waited, Revere occasionally took his eyes off the steeple to glance eastward, toward the menacing British fleet that hovered just outside Boston Harbor. Looking in that direction, he would likely have seen the beacon of the lighthouse on Little Brewster Island. Ironically, that light was probably far more important to the cause of American independence than the one Revere would shortly see in the Old North Church steeple.

ONE *if by* SEA

Built in 1716, the harbor lighthouse had guided countless thousands of trading ships to the Boston wharves and, in this way, contributed mightily to the prosperity of the colonies. That same prosperity had convinced the British that their upstart colonists should pay for the protection of King George's fleet and other expensive services rendered by the mother country. So Parliament decided to tax the colonies. American businessmen, who to this day have never smiled at the thought of taxes, responded hostilely, even to the Parliament's penny-a-pound tax on tea. In Boston, a party of anti-tax demonstrators painted their faces, dressed up like Indians—another long-lived trait of Americans is their active sense of humor—and dumped a shipload of Chinese tea into the harbor. The British retaliated by blockading Boston with their fleet. After that events moved swiftly. Massachusetts city dwellers and farmers started hoarding gunpowder and calling themselves Minutemen. People began to talk openly about independence from England, and, having seen a light in a church steeple, Revere found himself riding through the night toward Lexington.

Meanwhile, the British had taken over the lighthouse and were operating it themselves as a beacon for their ships. To strike back at the blockading fleet, the Minutemen decided to put out the light. Early in July 1775 a small detachment of American troops landed on Little Brewster Island, removed the oil and lantern, and set fire to the lighthouse. To observers on the mainland, the burning tower seemed a great torch "ascending up to Heaven." The flames confused gunners on the British warships, who tried but failed to blast the Minutemen out of the water as they retreated back to Boston.

But damage to the lighthouse was not as complete as the Americans might have hoped. The scorched walls of the tower had barely cooled before the British put workmen ashore on Little Brewster to begin repairs. A contingent of royal marines stood guard while the carpenters sawed lumber and pounded nails.

News of the rapidly progressing repair work soon reached Boston, where General George Washington had recently taken over command of the American (Continental) Army. Washington felt that he could not allow the tower to be relighted and decided to send a second raiding party to the island. On July 30 some 300 Continental soldiers, led by Major Benjamin Tupper, set out for Little Brewster in whaleboats. Aided by darkness, the Americans caught the redcoat marines by surprise and defeated them. They destroyed the work of the British carpenters, set fire to everything that would burn, and escaped thanks to the timely fire of an artillery piece on nearby Nantasket Head.

The Americans lost only one soldier in the fight, while their opponents suffered heavy casualties. Washington called the raiders "gallant and soldier-like" and praised them for so adroitly "possessing themselves of the enemie's post at the lighthouse."

Although the harbor was now dark and unsafe for nighttime navigation, the British fleet did not leave. Several of the king's warships remained near the harbor entrance, harassing fishermen and threatening coastal towns and villages. The continued presence of enemy vessels in the harbor enraged Massachusetts patriots, especially Samuel Adams, the Boston firebrand who had more or less invented the American Revolution in the first place. Unable to stomach the sight of the British ships, Adams devised a plan to force them out of the harbor. The effectiveness of the gun at Nantasket Head during Tupper's raid on the lighthouse may have suggested the scheme. The Americans would land troops on Nantasket Head and various strategic islands in the harbor, fortify them, and drive the blockaders away with artillery.

On June 13, 1776, only three weeks before the former colonies officially declared their independence from Britain, armed boats once more set sail from Boston and headed for the outer harbor. By dawn on the following day, the American gunners had their cannon ready, and the pounding began. The king's sailors woke up to a hot rain of shot and shell, and soon they had sails set and were racing for the high seas.

But before weighing anchor, one of the British ships put a landing party ashore on Little Brewster Island. The sailors hurriedly stacked gunpowder inside the lighthouse tower, lit a slow-burning fuse, and ran for their boats. While rowing back to their ship, they heard a thunderous explosion and watched the mortally wounded tower collapse into the sea. The Boston Light, it would seem, had few friends during the Revolutionary War.

*O**ne of several lights near Gloucester, the Eastern Point Lighthouse marks the entrance to the town's bustling harbor. Built in 1832 and replaced in 1890 by a larger brick tower and a wood-frame keeper's residence, the station still looks much as it did a century ago. The light continues to be seen each evening, it's powerful beacon flashing once every five seconds.*

PORTSMOUTH HARBOR LIGHT

Portsmouth, New Hampshire – 1771, 1804, and 1877

Colonial governments had very little money to spend on public works and were generally stingy with navigational improvements such as lighthouses. In New Hampshire, the first navigational light was so modest that it was not really a lighthouse at all. Each night, beginning in April 1771, a keeper hoisted a small lantern to the top of the flagpole at Fort William and Mary, on the banks of the Piscataqua River. Eventually, the New Hampshire legislature built a lighthouse on a narrow point of land beside the fort, but it is not clear when it went into operation. A wooden lighthouse tower already stood on the point in 1782 when Marquis de Lafayette, the famed Revolutionary War general, paid it a visit. A few years later Lafayette's good friend and comrade-in-arms George Washington also visited the lighthouse.

Keeper Titus Salter, an old sea captain, must have spent days washing windows and floors, buffing metal fittings, and polishing the buttons on his coat after he learned, in 1789, that the president himself would be knocking on his door. And knock he did. Washington came and, despite the polished buttons, went away four days later with a less-than-enthusiastic opinion of the keeper. Soon Salter started receiving uncomplimentary notes from the Secretary of the Treasury Alexander Hamilton, whom Washington had placed in charge of the nation's "Lighthouse Establishment." It is difficult to say whether Salter was really doing a poor job of keeping the light or just had political differences with the administration, but by 1792 he was gone.

Hamilton replaced Salter with a man named Moses McFarland, who was extremely anxious to secure the position, even though it paid only $3.46 a week. The job was no prize. McFarland found that he could barely feed his family of six on his low salary, and almost as serious a problem were the big guns at the adjacent fort, by then called Fort Constitution. Their thunder cracked walls and blew out the windows of the keeper's residence.

By 1804 the lighthouse had been replaced by an octagonal tower. When complete, it stood eighty feet above the water, and its lantern contained thirteen spherical reflectors, each fourteen inches in diameter. The new tower remained solid for nearly three quarters of a century. It was finally torn down in 1877 and replaced by a cast-iron tower with a lantern fifty feet above mean sea level. This tower still stands today, its fourth-order Fresnel lens guiding ships with a flashing green light visible for twelve miles.

HOW TO GET THERE:

From U.S. 1 in Portsmouth, follow signs to Fort Constitution, or take Route 1B and then Wentworth Road to the fort, which is now part of a Coast Guard base. Most of the base is off-limits, but the old colonial fort is open to the public. The best views of the light can be had from the fortress walls.

A ferry from Portsmouth carries visitors to the Isle of Shoals, location of another important New Hampshire lighthouse. Its light, flashing from a 58-foot granite tower, can be seen from 15 miles at sea. The keeper's dwelling serves as a bed and breakfast.

ISLES OF SHOALS LIGHT

White Island, New Hampshire – 1821 and 1859

Barren, rocky, swept by high winds, and pounded on all sides by towering waves, the Isles of Shoals are more a part of the ocean than of the land. Yet this tiny archipelago of islets, some of them no more than a few dozen yards across, was home to one of the earliest European settlements in North America. During the sixteenth century fishermen flocked here like seabirds to exploit the giant schools of cod that teemed in the waters off the coast. Homes, churches, and packing sheds clung tenuously to the rocks—until the Atlantic threw up a storm to smash them. Survivors would then settle down to the task of rebuilding their homes and lives.

The Isles of Shoals have long attracted the adventurous and hardy of spirit. During the mid-1800s Ralph Waldo Emerson visited the Appledore Hotel, a famed and gracious hostelry located on one of the Isles of Shoals' nine islands. Other guests included Nathaniel Hawthorne, William Mason, and John Greenleaf Whittier. The Old Appledore Hotel fell into ruin long ago; all but a few traces of it are gone. Yet plenty of summer visitors still come here. A research station operated by Cornell University and the University of New Hampshire draws students and scientists who study the unique environment and wildlife of the islands. There is also a nondenominational church camp operated by Unitarian-Univeralists.

A lighthouse has stood on White Island—one of the Isles' more barren outcroppings—since 1821. The original stone tower stood eighty-two feet tall and served until just before the Civil War. In 1859 it was replaced by a shorter brick tower, its walls built two feet thick to help them survive the Atlantic's pounding waves. On more than one occasion, prodigious storms have swept the island, their thundering surf driving keepers into the tower for refuge. Today the station is uninhabited, its powerful light automated.

HOW TO GET THERE:

White Island, in the Isles of Shoals chain, is accessible only by private boat. The automated light station is closed to the public; however, it is possible to get an excellent view of the lighthouse from the Isles of Shoals Ferry. During warm-weather months the ferry leaves from Baker Wharf on Market Street in Portsmouth. For schedules and other information, call Isles of Shoals Steamship Company at (800) 441–4620 or (603) 431–5500.

Barren rock provides a stark setting for Isles of Shoals Light Station, located several miles off Portsmouth, New Hampshire.

CAPE ANN LIGHT

Thacher Island, Massachusetts – 1771 and 1861

The Cape Ann Light station may once have saved the life of a president. Steaming home from Europe in 1919, the passenger liner *America* had on board a special guest, President Woodrow Wilson, returning from the Versailles Peace Conference, which officially ended World War I. Blinded by a heavy fog off the coast of Massachusetts, the *America*'s crew unknowingly had the big ship on a collision course with rocky Thacher Island, just off Cape Ann. The fog was so thick that no one saw the lights of the island's twin lighthouse towers. Then a sailor heard the blast of a foghorn, and the captain ordered an emergency change of course—just in time to avert a disaster of truly historic proportions.

No one knows how many ships and lives have been saved by the Cape Ann station since it was established more than two centuries ago by the Bay Council of colonial Massachusetts. A few years before the start of

Cape Ann Light on Thacher Island warns mariners against repeating the misfortune of Reverend Anthony Thacher. In 1635 Thacher was shipwrecked on the island that now bears his name. Nearly three centuries later the station likely saved President Woodrow Wilson from a similar fate.

the American Revolution, the council decided that too many good ships had been lost on the rocks of treacherous Thacher Island and that something must be done to warn mariners. The council determined to build not one, but a pair of lighthouses on the island. To secure land for the project, colonial officials bought the island from heirs of Reverend Anthony Thacher who was, ironically, the first man known to have been shipwrecked there.

Thacher had suffered profound personal tragedy in 1635, when an August hurricane swept over the ship on which he and his family were passengers. The storm spared Thacher and his wife, throwing them up onto the barren shores of what later would be known as Thacher Island. But everyone else on the ship perished, including the four Thacher children. To compensate the minister partially for his great loss, the colonial government gave him the island.

More than 135 years after the Thacher shipwreck, two stone towers stood on the island, their lanterns ninety feet above sea level. The colony hired as keeper a sea captain and notorious Tory named Kirkwood, who first lit the twin lamps on December 21, 1771. When the Revolution broke out a few years later, a party of Massachusetts Minutemen hustled Kirkwood off the island, and the lights were plunged into darkness until the end of the war.

Almost ninety years later, on the eve of another conflict—the Civil War—the Lighthouse Board rebuilt the old towers, raising them to a height of 124 feet above the rocks and 168 feet above the sea. When the work was completed in 1861, the board indicated the importance it placed on the Cape Ann Light station by fitting the lanterns of both towers with first-order Fresnel lenses. The northern light was discontinued in 1932, but it has since been reactivated by the Thacher Island Association.

Occasionally, lighthouse keepers have been saved by their own lights. On Christmas Eve in 1865, the assistant keeper at Cape Ann fell seriously ill. The station's keeper, a wounded and crippled Civil War veteran named Bray, felt he had no choice but to take the sick man to the mainland, where he could receive proper medical attention. While Bray was ashore, the sea was brewing a storm. When the keeper headed back toward Thacher Island in his small boat, he found himself rowing into the teeth of a blizzard. It was snowing so hard that Bray had no idea whether he was pulling toward the island or toward the open sea. To miss the island meant almost certain death, and for a time Bray thought that was exactly what he had done. Then he saw the glow of two familiar lights. The keeper's wife and children had struggled through deep snowdrifts to keep the lamps burning. Bray pointed his boat toward the lights and put his back into the oars. Later, sitting at the table in his warm house and surrounded by his family, the keeper may have thought he had never tasted such a good Christmas dinner.

HOW TO GET THERE:

The twin lights on Thacher Island can be seen from the backshore areas of Gloucester on the mainland. Lands End in Rockport offers a particularly fine view. During the summer some boat services in Rockport and Gloucester provide excursions to Thacher Island.

BAKER'S ISLAND LIGHT

Salem, Massachusetts – 1798

During the War of 1812, civilian lighthouse keeper Joseph Perkins joined the U.S. Navy for a single thrilling afternoon. While keeping watch from his station on Baker's Island, Perkins spotted a pair of large British warships bearing down on the American frigate *Constitution,* which lay just outside Salem Harbor. Outnumbered and outgunned, the captain of the *Constitution* wanted to avoid a battle and hoped to slip inside the harbor, where there were shore guns to drive away the British. But he seemed unable to find a safe channel into the harbor. Instantly sizing up the situation, Perkins jumped into a boat, rowed out to the American ship, and offered his services as helmsman. Perkins knew the channels here as well as any sailor in Massachusetts. After piloting "Old Ironsides" to the safety of Salem Harbor and frustrating the British, Perkins returned to his workaday chores at the Baker's Island Lighthouse.

Established in 1789, the Baker's Island light station originally displayed two lights. Like the original Matinicus Rock station in Maine, the lighthouse consisted of two towers connected by a keeper's dwelling. But during an early nineteenth-century economy drive, Treasury officials decided the island needed only one light and darkened the lantern in the second tower. Then, in 1817, the giant freighter *Union* slammed into the island, spilling tons of pepper and tin into the surf. Survivors of the wreck claimed that they had mistaken the Baker's Island station, which now displayed only one light, for the single-towered Boston Light on Little Brewster Island.

Spurred by a public outcry, the government reactivated the second light, and Baker's Island remained a double-light station for another fifty years. Under orders from the Lighthouse Board, keepers finally snuffed out the second light in 1870, and it has remained dark ever since. But the other Baker's Island beacon still burns, more than a century after its companion became a "darkhouse." The light guides ships with alternating white and red flashes spaced about seven seconds apart.

A single lighthouse tower now dominates rocky Baker's Island. The light in a companion tower was snuffed out in 1870. (Courtesy U.S. Coast Guard)

HOW TO GET THERE:

Located on a small, isolated island in the Atlantic, this lighthouse is difficult to reach. It is most easily seen from the water or the air.

Once known as the "Venice of the New World," Salem sent whole fleets of trading ships to India, China, and the West Indies. When these "Indiamen" returned, fortunes were made on the spices, sugar, molasses, coffee, tea, and chinaware that poured out of their holds. Salem's cleverest trader was Elias Derby, who was probably America's first millionaire. Although not a seaman himself, Derby knew how to make money on shipping ventures, and he swelled his profits by investing in construction of the enormous wharf that now bears his name. Only twenty-five feet tall, the diminutive Derby Wharf Lighthouse has marked the end of the wharf since 1871. The lamp in its tiny lantern room once burned whale oil. Today, its flashing red signal is powered by a solar panel and batteries.

MARBLEHEAD LIGHT

Salem, Massachusetts – 1836 and 1895

Development has been an enemy of lighthouses, especially in this century. Newly constructed seaside hotels and other tall buildings have obscured beacons, forcing officials to move or even discontinue some light stations. Among the first lighthouses to be walled in by adjacent buildings was the small harbor light on Marblehead near Salem. Built in 1836 for $4,500, the squat Marblehead tower was not much taller than an ordinary house. It served effectively for many years, but by 1880 two- and three-story cottages had sprouted like weeds all around the station, so much so that helmsmen trying to steer their vessels into Salem Harbor could no longer see the light at all.

As a temporary remedy, the keeper anchored a one-hundred-foot mast firmly in the ground, and each night he hoisted a lantern to the top. Eventually, this inadequate arrangement drew so many complaints from sailors that the Lighthouse Board approved a new tower for Marblehead. By 1895 work crews had completed the structure, a skeleton tower poised on eight iron legs. With its lantern 105 feet above the ground and 130 feet above the harbor, it raised the light far above the cottages that besieged the old lighthouse. The iron tower still stands today, exhibiting a fixed green light.

During the great New England Hurricane of 1938, the station's electric power failed, but keeper Harry Marden responded quickly to the emergency. Bringing his car to the tower, he hooked cables to the battery and kept the light burning.

HOW TO GET THERE:

From U.S. 1, take Route 114 to Marblehead. Turn right onto Ocean Avenue, which ends near the lighthouse. A small park here provides benches and an excellent view of the water and of summer sunsets. The lighthouse is closed to the public.

A summer day ends with a splash of color at Marblehead Lighthouse. One of the few skeleton towers in New England, the lighthouse stands, as spiders do, on eight legs.

BOSTON LIGHT

Boston Harbor, Massachusetts – 1716 and 1783

A sheet of paper posted on the wall of the Boston Lighthouse contains a long and extraordinary list of names. The first name on the list is that of George Worthylake, whose tragic story is told on page 2. Then come the names of the other sixty men who have served as keepers of North America's oldest and most storied light station. Consider this: The Boston Light has had half again as many keepers as the United States has had presidents. Like Worthylake, who lasted three years, some keepers stayed only a short time at the light.

But others, such as Robert Ball, who kept the light from 1733 to 1774, held the job for decades, much longer than any president has held office.

The Boston Light is much older than the nation it now serves. Built in 1716 by the colony of Massachusetts, it was the first true lighthouse, with tower and glassed-in lantern, in North America. To defray the expense of maintaining the light, colonial officials imposed a duty of one penny per ton on ships moving in and out of Boston Harbor. Early keepers, including Worthylake, 1716–18, and John Hayes, 1718–33, received a salary of fifty to seventy British pounds per year, which they supplemented by serving as harbor pilots.

In 1719 Hayes asked "that a great Gun be placed on the Said Island to answer Ships in a Fogg." Colonial officials liked the suggestion and brought a cannon to the island. No doubt to his chagrin, Hayes received no additional pay for firing the gun whenever fog socked in the harbor. The old cannon has survived the centuries and is now on display at the U.S. Coast Guard Academy in New London, Connecticut.

Hayes almost lost three years' salary in 1720 when a lamp overturned in the lantern, causing serious fire damage to the tower. Assuring his superiors that "ye said fire was not occasioned by ye least neglect of ye Memorialist," Hayes managed to beat back an attempt to make him pay the 216 pounds needed for repairs.

The violence of the American Revolution left only ruins on Little Brewster Island, and in 1783 the Massachusetts legislature raised 1,450 pounds to rebuild the lighthouse. For their money, the people of Massachusetts got a solid structure with walls seventy-five feet high and more than seven feet thick at the base. The tower has stood for more than 200 years, through countless gales, half a dozen hurricanes, and an assortment of fires and other calamities, all without substantial repair.

To make the light more effective, the Lighthouse Board had fourteen feet added to the height of the tower in 1859. The second-order Fresnel lens installed that same year is still in use. Today it focuses on a 1,800,000-candlepower light, visible for up to sixteen miles. In inclement weather, the keepers of Boston Light continued to fire their fog cannon right up until 1850, when it was replaced by an enormous bell. Later the station employed the strongest available trumpets, sirens, and horns to warn ships.

Despite the great power of the station's light and the strength of its fog signals, a number of ships have been lost practically within shouting distance of the lighthouse. In December 1839 three hurricanes struck Boston Harbor in less than two weeks, driving scores of vessels, including the schooner *Charlotte* and the bark

Dennis Dever, one of North America's last lighthouse keepers, kept the 135-year-old, second-order Fresnel lens sparkling using ordinary window cleaner. The brass frame and prisms were crafted in Paris.

Lloyd, onto rocks near the light. In 1861 the 991-ton square-rigger *Maritana* got caught in a blinding snowstorm in Massachusetts Bay and slammed into Shag Rocks, a short distance from Boston Light. Dozens drowned or were crushed to death when the big wooden ship broke in half. Using a small dory, lighthouse personnel rescued twelve survivors who had floated to Shag Rocks on fragments of the ship. In 1882 the Shag Rocks also claimed the *Fanny Pike,* but the keeper managed to rescue the entire crew. The schooner *Calvin F. Baker* hit rocks and sank near the lighthouse during a storm in 1898. Before help could arrive, three crewmen froze to death in the rigging. On Christmas Day 1909 the coal schooner *Davis Palmer* slammed into Finn's Ledge and went down with all hands. It is said that Captain Leroy Kowen's wife had Christmas dinner on the stove when a friend arrived with the awful news. Fate was kinder to the crew of the USS *Alacrity,* a Navy ship that hit rocks just off Little Brewster Island on February 3, 1918. The *Alacrity* sank, but its twenty-four half-frozen crewmen were rescued by keeper Charles Jennings, who had to push his dory over ice and through freezing surf to reach the wreck.

According to legend, none of the station's fog signals has ever effectively penetrated the mysterious area known as the "Ghost Walk," several miles east of the lighthouse. For reasons that are still not thoroughly understood, sailors caught in the Ghost Walk cannot hear the signal. A team of students from the Massachusetts Institute of Technology lived on Little Brewster for the entire summer of 1893 trying out one experimental foghorn after another. All of them failed to reach the Ghost Walk.

HOW TO GET THERE:

*N*orth America's oldest and most famous light-house cannot be reached by land. Boston Harbor tour boats often pass by Little Brewster Island, however, and offer an excellent view of the light. *For information call the Greater Boston Area Visitors Center at (617) 536–4100.*

*G*ray and weather-streaked, the stone lighthouse tower on Graves Ledge looks very old, but its appearance is deceiving. Commissioned in 1905, it numbers among the few New England light stations established in this century. Some think that Graves Ledge received its rather ominous name because of tragedies such as the one that befell the Mary O'Hara and her crew in 1941. During a blizzard in January of that year, nineteen of those onboard the schooner O'Hara drowned or froze to death after she rammed a barge anchored near the Graves Light. Actually, the ledge is named for Thomas Graves, a prominent sea trader from colonial Massachusetts.

MINOTS LEDGE LIGHT

Cohasset, Massachusetts – 1850 and 1860

Few navigational obstacles have destroyed as many ships and lives as Minots Ledge, a narrow, barely visible outcropping of rock just off Cohasset, Massachusetts. A survey compiled in 1847 by lighthouse inspector I. W. P. Lewis listed dozens of barks, brigs, coasters, ketches, schooners, and large ships torn apart by the ledge. At least forty lives have been snuffed out in these wrecks, and Lewis estimated property damage of more than $360,000.

Although government officials had long recognized the dangers of the ledge, none had ever seriously suggested building a lighthouse there. The feat was thought

Seeming totally at the mercy of the sea, Minots Ledge Lighthouse still has a firm grip on the submerged rocks beneath it, after more than 130 years. Interlocking granite blocks, some weighing two tons, help it resist giant waves.

to be impossible. Any lighthouse on Minots Ledge would be exposed to the full force of the ocean. How long would it stand in a winter gale?

But Lewis was convinced that something had to be done, and, armed with his survey, he forced the hand of Treasure Department Fifth Auditor Stephen Pleasonton, the country's top lighthouse official. A tightfisted conservative, Pleasonton was highly suspicious of new ideas, especially if they cost money. But in this case, Pleasonton decided to take a chance and approved plans for a radical new lighthouse design, one that showed promise of surviving the punishments of Minots Ledge.

Instead of the usual solid cylinder, the tower would consist of nine iron pilings, each of them sunk five feet into the rock and cemented in place. The keeper's dwelling and lantern would perch atop the legs, some seventy-five feet above the ravaging ocean. In theory, the tower's reinforced legs would offer little resistance to the wind and water, and even the most formidable ocean waves would pass right through the open superstructure.

The U.S. Topographical Department itself designed and built the skeleton lighthouse, for this was no small feat of engineering and construction. Crews worked from a schooner anchored beside the ledge, and more than once the ocean swept drill rigs and other equipment off the rocks. The work took three years and a great deal of money to complete, with a grimacing Pleasonton signing the checks. Finally, on New Year's Day in 1850, the lamps at the top of the spidery lighthouse were lit.

Captain William Smith, who designed and supervised construction of the lighthouse, proclaimed that it could weather "any storm without danger." But Isaac Dunham, the station's first keeper, did not share his confidence. Dunham, who could feel the new lighthouse swaying in the wind and hear its legs groan under the stress of constant pounding by waves, had grave doubts about the safety of the structure. Following a series of particularly violent autumn storms that "would have frightened Daniel Webster," Dunham quit the post. Dunham's resignation, after just nine months as keeper, may well have saved his life. A few months after Dunham got his feet back on solid ground, a monumental gale bowled over the lighthouse, carrying two assistant keepers to their deaths (see page 4).

The tragedy had an unexpected casualty: It may very well have focused the attention of congressmen on Plea-

sonton's spotty, thirty-year record as administrator of the Lighthouse Service. A congressional panel, convened during the spring of 1851, at about the time of the Minots Ledge disaster, found the nation's navigational aids in terrible shape. Pleasonton had allowed so little money to trickle through to the service that lighthouse walls were cracking and towers literally toppling into the sea. The panel learned that Pleasonton had ignored the highly effective French-made Fresnel lenses in favor of the outdated reflectors designed by his friend, Winslow Lewis. (Interestingly, Winslow Lewis was the grandfather of lighthouse inspector I. W. P. Lewis, mentioned earlier.) No suggestion was made that Pleasonton had any pecuniary interest in ordering the service to use Lewis reflectors, and no such charge has ever been proven. But Congress took a dim view of the decision. Ultimately, Congress took administration of the service away from Pleasonton and placed it in the hands of a new Lighthouse Board consisting largely of engineers and mariners.

As one of its first tasks, the board undertook reconstruction of the Minots Ledge Lighthouse. The effort consumed eight years and more than $330,000, but by August 1860, the new tower was complete. This time the tower was built with granite blocks laid in parallel courses atop foundation stones weighing two tons each. In this case, at least, stone has proven stronger than iron: The lighthouse still stands, nearly 140 years after its construction. Giant waves have actually swept over the top of the ninety-seven-foot tower, breaking windows but causing no serious structural damage.

The lantern delivers a distinctive warning to mariners: one white flash, followed by four flashes, followed by three more. The one-four-three rhythm reminds lovers of the words *I love you,* and Minots Ledge is known to the more romantically inclined as the "I Love You" light.

HOW TO GET THERE:

The lighthouse is closed to the public and cannot be reached by land. It can, however, be seen from several points along the coast near Cohasset. Boaters headed north or south along the Massachusetts coast have an excellent view of the light.

Although built in 1811, the sloping, octagonal walls and birdcage lantern of the Scituate Light tower in Massachusetts give it a strikingly modern appearance. Deactivated in 1860, the old lighthouse has served more years of disuse than most lighthouses have been in operation. (Courtesy Bob and Sandra Shanklin)

LIGHTHOUSES OF CAPE COD

Cape Cod (Highland) – 1798 and 1857

Race Point – 1816

Long Point – 1827

Nauset Beach – 1838 and 1923

Nobska – 1828 and 1876

Like a whirlpool of sand in the ocean, Cape Cod sweeps seaward from the far southeast corner of Massachusetts, arching to the north and finally curling back on itself about twenty miles due east of Plymouth. Deposited by glaciers that blanketed New England during much of the last 100,000 years, the sands of the cape are constantly on the move, wearing away in one area and building up in another. Land has only a tenuous hold on this place; the ocean seems always poised to rush in and reclaim the cape as its own.

But to mariners sailing westward out of the broad Atlantic, the high dunes of Cape Cod have always been a substantial and welcome sight. The Pilgrims first landed here in 1620, before sailing across Cape Cod Bay to step off onto Plymouth Rock. Once they had spotted the cape, the captains of clipper ships headed back from Europe, Africa, or China knew that Boston Harbor waited less than half a day's sail to the west. A sizable number of rugged New England whalers once called the cape home, just as many fishermen do today.

But if the cape is a friend of sailors, it is also a threat. As a point of land extending far out into the Atlantic, the cape is a formidable navigational obstacle that has ruined many good ships and killed many strong men. Four centuries of wrecks have filled the sands of its beaches with bits and pieces of vessels now long forgotten.

Cape Cod is just the sort of place where you would expect to find lighthouses, and, indeed, it boasts several major lights. Most prominent is the Cape Cod Light, also known as the Highland Light. The tower stands on a high bluff near Truro, and its beacon, situated 183 feet above the sea, can be seen for up to twenty-three miles. For sailors emerging from the dark reaches of the Atlantic, Cape Cod Light is often the first visual evidence that the North American continent is near.

Soon after the first Cape Cod tower was built in 1798, sailors began to confuse the light with the fixed beacon of the Boston Light, forty-one miles to the northwest. To solve this problem, a rotating opaque screen was placed in the lantern. Completing one revolution every eight minutes, the screen was supposed to make the light flash. But, as one grumbling mariner was quick to point out, the screen partially obscured the light much of the time and gave it "phases, like [those of] the moon." Said he: "There are circumstances enough, at sea, to obscure the best of lights without any

The first Cape Cod (Highland) Lighthouse was built in 1798. This one dates to 1857.

contrivances on shore to assist this misfortune." Objections notwithstanding, the screen system was retained for many years.

The Lighthouse Board rebuilt the old Highland tower in 1857, fitting it with a first-order Fresnel lens. Rotating on a reservoir of mercury, the bull's-eye lens concentrated light into flashes of nearly 200,000 candlepower. When the station's oil lamps were replaced by a 1,000-watt electric bulb in 1932, the strength of the flash was increased to an incredible 4,000,000 candlepower. The Highland Light remains one of the most powerful in North America, although today, it employs a dual electric beacon similar to those used at airports.

Henry David Thoreau made several visits to the Cape Cod Lighthouse during the mid-1800s. Noting rapid erosion of the sandy cliff beneath the tower, Thoreau wondered how long the lighthouse could remain on its precarious perch. Today the edge of the cliff is only thirty feet from the base of the tower. Many believe that unless it is moved, the lighthouse will soon topple over into the Atlantic.

Hundreds of ships have ended their days on Race Point, which forms Cape Cod's westward knuckle. Vessels must round the point to reach Provincetown Harbor a few miles to the southeast, and over the years more than a few have tried but failed. No one knows exactly how many ships have piled up on the sands of the point, but more than a hundred wrecks have been noted there since the establishment of the Race Point Light in 1816. No doubt countless others have been saved by the light's flashing white beacon, which can be seen from a distance of twelve miles.

Established in 1827 near the end of a sandy spit where the cape nearly completes a 360-degree inward spiral, Long Point Light still serves Provincetown Harbor with its flashing green light. During the Civil War authorities

Looking like a rook on a chessboard, Long Point Lighthouse (top right) marks the end of a sandy arm of land curving back toward Provincetown on Cape Cod. The panels outside the lantern convert sunlight to electricity to power the lamp. Imperiled by an eroding shoreline, Nauset Beach Lighthouse (bottom right) faces certain doom unless moved soon to higher ground.

From a serene perch, the Nobska Lighthouse warns sailors away from two treacherous shoals below.

lens throws out a 28,000-candlepower light visible from sixteen miles out at sea. The light flashes once every six seconds. Sailors nearing the shoals see a red light, while those in safe water see a white light.

responded quickly to rumors of an impending attack by Confederate warships, building a pair of small earthen gun batteries near the lighthouse on Long Point. The tiny Confederate Navy was never really up to such an expedition, however, and citizens of Provincetown soon dubbed the two batteries "Fort Harmless" and "Fort Useless."

The Nauset Beach Light, first lighted in 1838, guards Cape Cod's Atlantic coast south of the Cape Cod Light. Originally, the Nauset station displayed three lights shining from identical towers known to many locals as the "Three Sisters of Nauset." Eventually, the government determined that one light would serve just as well as three, whereupon two of Nauset's iron maidens suffered the indignity of being sold and converted for use as summer cottages. A new tower was erected in 1923 and guides ships with alternating red and white flashes.

In Woods Hole at the cape's far southwestern tip, the Nobska Light warns ships away from a pair of vicious shoals called the Hedge Fence and L'Hommedieu. The first lighthouse here, built in 1828, was a simple stone cottage with a lantern on top, but in 1876, the Lighthouse Board approved a new tower for the Nobska station. An iron shell was built in Chelsea, Massachusetts, and shipped to the cape in four sections. Work crews at Nobska erected the shell and lined it with brick. The tower stands forty-two feet above the ground and eighty-seven feet above the sea. Its fourth-order Fresnel

HOW TO GET THERE:

Cape Cod (Highland) Light: *From U.S. 6 in Truro, take Highland Avenue and follow signs to the light. The lighthouse is not open to the public. Because of severe erosion, there is no access to the beach here.*

Race Point Light: *From U.S. 6 in Provincetown, take Race Point Road to Race Point Beach. A visit to this lighthouse is recommended only for veteran walkers. Two miles of soft sand separate the parking area from the light. The National Park Services closes this area to protect thousands of nesting terns during mating season, but they might just as well leave the area open; the terns have their own very effective means of keeping you at a distance. If you would prefer to avoid the long walk and the hostility of the terns, then substitute a visit to the informative Life Saving Museum near the beach.*

Long Point Light: *Take a short boat ride across the harbor from Provincetown. Rental boats and regular shuttles are available in Provincetown during the summer.*

Nauset Beach Light: *From U.S. 6, take Brackett Road and follow the signs to Nauset Beach. The light is closed to the public but can be seen from the National Seashore parking area. However, the original "Three Sisters," long out of service, have been reunited and can be visited with a short walk down a paved trail from the Nauset Light Beach parking lot.*

The four lighthouses listed above are all located within the Cape Cod National Seashore. Unauthorized vehicle and foot traffic contributes to the erosion that is eating up parts of the cape. Please enjoy, but do not destroy, this treasure. For more information about Cape Cod, call the National Seashore Headquarters at (508) 349–3785.

Nobska Light: *From Falmouth follow Woods Hole Road for 3 miles until it becomes Main Street in the village of Woods Hole. Turn left onto Church Street, which will take you to one of the most picturesque lighthouses in all of New England.*

LIGHTHOUSES OF NANTUCKET

Brant Point – 1746, 1759, and 1901

Great Point – 1784 and 1816

Nothing is more democratic than a New England town meeting. If a town is to part with so much as a dime, then a majority of the community must agree to spending it. And since no one wants to appear loose with their neighbors' money, the budgets that emerge from town meetings are notoriously tight-fisted. So it is ironic that North America's second-oldest light station owes its existence to a town meeting held on Nantucket Island on January 24, 1746. On that day the sea captains of the island addressed their fellow citizens and asked for a lighthouse to help them find the harbor. In a rare fit of fiscal openhandedness, the people of Nantucket offered to raise 200 English pounds for the project, and not long afterward, a little wooden lighthouse was built on Brant Point at the entrance to Nantucket Harbor. At the time only one other lighthouse stood in all of Britain's North American colonies: the stone-towered Boston Light on Little Brewster Island.

Unfortunately, the Brant Point Light would not have as distinguished a career as its big neighbor to the north. It burned to the ground only a dozen years after its construction. At another town meeting held the following year, citizens once again opened their purses, and money was raised for another tower. This one was knocked down by a windstorm in 1774. The *Massachusetts Gazette* reported: "We hear from Nantucket that on Wednesday the 9th of March,

Instant at about 8 o'clock, they had a most violent Gust of Wind that perhaps was ever known there, but it lasted only a minute. It seemed to come in a narrow Vein, and in its progress blew down and totally destroyed the Light-House on that Island besides several Shops, Barns, etc."

As many as ten lighthouses have stood on Nantucket's Brant Point since islanders built the first one here in 1746. This small tower has stood since 1901. (Courtesy U.S. Coast Guard)

The citizens of Nantucket then paid for yet another tower, which burned down in 1783. At this point the islanders may have felt they were throwing good money after bad, and the next light erected on Brant Point was nothing more than a lantern hoisted on a pole. Its light was so dim that sailors compared it to the glow of a lightning bug. Eventually, this unsatisfactory "bug light" was abandoned. Subsequent lights on the point were destroyed by storms, ruined by rot and salt water, condemned by inspectors, pulled down by the Lighthouse Board, and otherwise undone so that, in all, a total of ten lighthouses have stood there.

Perhaps surprisingly, the current lighthouse has survived since 1901. Its white cylindrical wooden tower raises its lantern only twenty-six feet above the water, making it the lowest light in New England. Focused by a fourth-order Fresnel lens, its red light can be seen from about ten miles away.

The Great Point Light on the opposite side of the island has been less exasperating for the local citizenry. Built in 1784, it burned down only once, in 1816. Better still, from the point of view of the islanders, the original tower was paid for by the Commonwealth of Massachusetts, and its replacement, completed in 1816, by the U.S. government. Built of stone, the 1816 tower stood just over seventy feet tall. It displayed a fixed white light visible from about fourteen miles at sea. Sailors approaching the dangerous Cross Rip or Tuckernuck shoals saw a red light.

Nantucket's Great Point Lighthouse looked like this during the 1970s. This tower was knocked down by a storm and has recently been replaced by another, similar in appearance. (Courtesy U.S. Coast Guard)

HOW TO GET THERE:

The charming island of Nantucket can be reached by auto ferry from New Bedford, Falmouth, and Hyannis Port. In most cases, reservations are required. For ferry information and reservations, call Hi-Line Cruise in Hyannis Port at (508) 775–7185 or the Massachusetts Steamship Authority in Falmouth at (508) 548–3788. The ferries provide an excellent view of both lighthouses.

GAY HEAD LIGHT

Martha's Vineyard, Massachusetts – 1799 and 1856

Of the several lighthouses on Martha's Vineyard, the oldest and best known is the Gay Head Light. The headland takes its name from the bright colors streaking its cliffs. The tower built atop the cliffs in 1799 took advantage of their considerable height to raise its lantern 160 feet above the sea. To manage this lofty light station, the government hired a man with the unlikely name of Ebenezer Skiff. As it turned out, Skiff had a gift for gab, and at least twice during his career at Gay Head, he managed to talk his superiors into granting him a substantial raise. Few lighthouse keepers in that era ever accomplished such a feat.

The original Gay Head Lighthouse had an eight-sided wooden tower rising fifty-one feet above the cliff tops on a stone foundation. The Lighthouse Board ordered construction of a new tower in 1856, and this time the builder used brick. A first-order Fresnel lens focused the light, which could be seen from a distance of nineteen miles. The huge first-order lens has been replaced, but the light still throws out its distinct com-bination of three white flashes and one red flash every forty seconds.

Martha's Vineyard also boasts lighthouses at East Chop, West Chop, Edgartown, and Cape Poge, located on the northeastern point of Chappaquidick Island. When eroding cliffs threatened the Cape Poge Light in 1987, it was lifted by a sky crane and moved back some 500 feet.

HOW TO GET THERE:

During the summer the delightful island of Martha's Vineyard can be reached by auto ferry from several points in southern Massachusetts. For departures from New Bedford, call (508) 997–1688; from Falmouth, call (508) 548–3788; and from Hyannis Port, call (508) 775–7185. The Gay Head lighthouse is about 15 miles west of Edgartown or the Vineyard Haven ferry slips and can be reached by paved road.

Built atop a high cliff, Gay Head Lighthouse on Martha's Vineyard throws its light seaward from a point 160 feet above the water. (Courtesy U.S. Coast Guard)

With the soaring masts of antique sailing ships as a background, the Mystic Seaport Lighthouse coaxes visitors back into the eighteenth and nineteenth centuries. The lighthouse is a copy of the one at Brant Point on Nantucket.

CHAPTER FOUR

Lights of
THE LIBERTY LADIES
RHODE ISLAND and CONNECTICUT

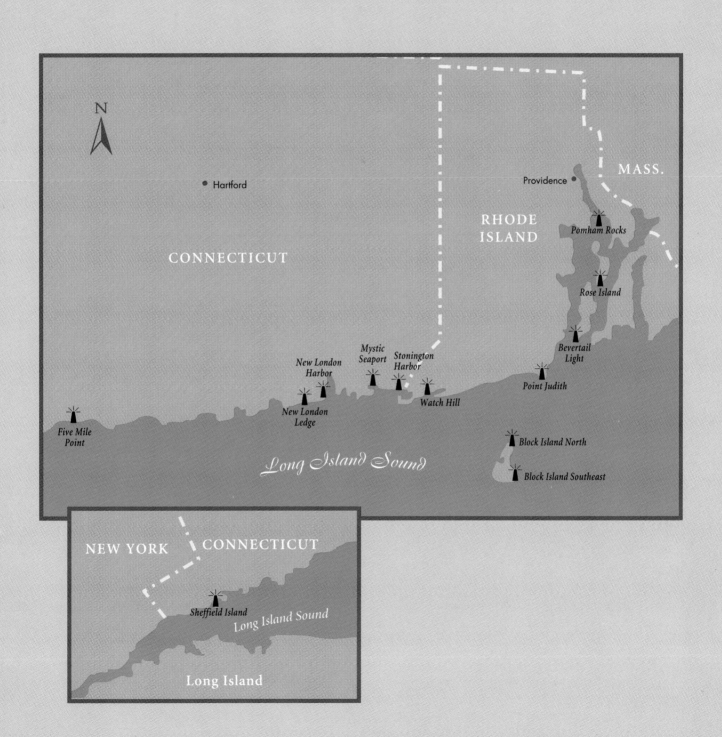

HARPER'S WEEKLY.

A JOURNAL OF CIVILIZATION

Vol. XIII.—No. 657.] NEW YORK, SATURDAY, JULY 31, 1869. [SINGLE COPIES, TEN CENTS. $4.00 PER YEAR IN ADVANCE.

Entered according to Act of Congress, in the Year 1869, by Harper & Brothers, in the Clerk's Office of the District Court of the United States, for the Southern District of New York.

The only lighthouse keeper to appear on the cover of Harper's Weekly, *the* Life Magazine *of its day, was Ida Lewis. Her rescues in Newport Harbor won her national acclaim and dozens of marriage proposals.*

*W*hen Ulysses S. Grant stepped out of his spotless presidential launch one summer day in 1869, he missed Lime Rock altogether and ended up standing ankle deep in Newport Harbor. The scene is easy to imagine: horrified aides and stout young sailors in immaculate uniforms piling over the side of the boat and splashing through the shallow water to the president's side and the old, bearded soldier waving them all back with his cane. Grant had gotten his feet wet plenty of times before—in the trenches at Richmond and Petersburg—and saw no reason now to let a little harmless seawater stop him short of his objective.

"I have come to see Ida Lewis," said the president. "To see her I'd get wet up to my armpits."

President Grant was certainly neither the first nor the last man to ruin his shoes in order to see a lady. But he was probably the first U.S. president to do so while on his way to visit a lady lighthouse keeper.

Miss Lewis graciously received Grant and just as graciously ignored his squishing shoes. She took his arm and led him on a tour of her tiny island, only a few times larger in area than the lighthouse itself. She showed him the workings of the light. She told him about life on Lime Rock, and he, perhaps, told her about his campaigns in the South. Their chat was warm, friendly, almost matter-of-fact. And why not? It was only natural the two should meet. Having just moved into the White House and still basking in the popular glow of his victories over the Confederates in Virginia, Grant was the best-known man in America. And Ida Lewis was her country's most famous woman.

THE LADY *of* LIME ROCK

At the time of Grant's visit in 1869, Ida Lewis was twenty-seven years old. She had already lived on Lime Rock for a dozen years and saved the lives of more than a dozen people. Sketches of her attractive face and trim figure had appeared in magazines and newspapers all over the country, along with sensational stories about her rescues and other exploits. She had become a national heroine, a kind of nineteenth-century starlet, and all without ever leaving Newport or traveling more than a mile or two from her rock.

When she was born in 1842, her parents weighed her down with the name Idawalley Zorada, but she would bear this burden handily, along with many others, in a life that lasted only one season less than seven decades. Her father was Captain Hosea Lewis, a Revenue-Cutter pilot who was retired to the supposedly more sedentary Lighthouse Service because of ill health. While Ida was still in her early teens, Captain Lewis became so sick that she and her mother were forced to take over the running of the Lime Rock Light. In addition to her duties at the lighthouse, Ida also rowed her younger sisters and brother back and forth to school each day. She made her daily trip to Newport regardless of gales or blizzards, and on more than one occasion, when she returned to her home on the rock, she was forced to cut her frozen stockings off her legs with a knife.

Sometimes storms caught Ida and the other Lewis children in the harbor in their open boat. Watching Ida pull against the waves with the oars, Captain Lewis felt especially helpless. "I have watched until I could bear it no longer," he said, "expecting every moment to see them swamped and the crew at the mercy of the waves. . . . Old sailor that I am . . . I could not endure to see them perish and realize that [I was] powerless to save them." But as the old seaman would eventually realize, his children were as safe with Ida as they would have been with anyone.

In the fall of 1858, at the age of sixteen, Ida glanced out the window of the lighthouse and saw an overturned sailboat and four young men desperately flailing at the cold harbor water. In a blink she had the station lifeboat out of the boathouse and was cutting smartly toward the scene of the accident. As any boys might have been, the four were deeply ashamed of having been rescued by a girl and the story of their rescue by young Ida Lewis was not widely known until many years later. Weeden King, one of the young men she rescued, later became Lieutenant King of the Union Army. Three years after surviving the near disaster in Newport Harbor, King lost his life in the much more tragic calamity of Bull Run.

In 1867 three negligent laborers allowed a prized sheep belonging to their employer to run off toward the harbor. Before they could catch the woolly creature, it fell into the harbor and was swept by the tide out toward Narragansett Bay. Fearing for their jobs, the men jumped into the keeper's skiff and pulled hard for the foundering sheep. But none of the three was an experienced waterman; a wave rolled them over, and they found themselves treading water along with the sheep. Again, Ida Lewis came to the rescue—this time of men who had stolen a boat belonging to her own family. When she got the men ashore, she turned back toward the bay and saved the unfortunate sheep as well.

Ida Lewis effected several more dramatic rescues, but the one that earned her nationwide fame took place in a winter gale on March 29, 1869. She was sick with a severe cold at the time and had huddled beside the kitchen stove much of the day, her shoes off and a blanket thrown over her shoulders. Late in the day her mother cried out to her. The big waves churned up by the storm had thrown over a boat in the harbor, and men were drowning. Although her mother tried to stop her, Ida ran for the lifeboat. With no shoes and her stockinged feet immersed in freezing water, she fought off one big wave after another. If she had reached the capsized boat only a few moments later, two numb and exhausted soldiers struggling nearby would have slipped under the water. Ida pulled them aboard, but this rescue would not be a complete success. Although she rowed in circles and called out, the boy who had piloted the soldiers' boat did not answer. He was gone forever.

The story of this exploit reached the pages of most of the major newspapers in the country. Engraved pictures of Ida and her Lime Rock Lighthouse were published in *Leslie's* magazine and in *Harper's Weekly*. Suddenly, she started receiving barrels of mail and visits from the rich, powerful, and famous. The Astors, Belmonts, and Vanderbilts all made social calls at the rock, as did President Grant, Vice President Schuyler Colfax, and General William Tecumseh Sherman. People gave her boats, medals, and gifts of money. She got offers from agents who wanted to put her on the stage. But she remained on Lime Rock with her family and her lighthouse.

Sandwiched into the stacks of mail that ended up on the lighthouse kitchen table day after day were more than a few marriage proposals. Men from every corner of the country sent her trinkets and dried flowers and asked for her hand. But the only proposal she ever accepted was that of William Wilson, a sometime fisherman and yacht captain who once moored his vessel near the rock. Their marriage was unhappy, however, and the restless sailor soon put to sea. Although she never saw Wilson again, she had only one answer to those who suggested she divorce him: "Whom God has joined together let no man put asunder."

Perhaps Wilson is not altogether to blame for the failure of his marriage to Ida. Maybe he felt that she could never really be his wife since she was already married to the Lime Rock Lighthouse. Like her legal marriage to Wilson, the latter union lasted until her death in 1911. When her father died in 1872, she was officially appointed assistant keeper, and after her mother's death seven years later, she became keeper. In all, she tended the light for more than half a century. When the sad news came on October 24, 1911, that Ida Lewis had died, the bells of vessels in Newport Harbor tolled through the night.

Ida Lewis was only one of thousands of women who found it their calling in life to turn lighthouses into lighthomes. Some were married to keepers or were the helpful daughters of lighthousemen. Others were keepers themselves. Whatever their title or status, these tough women endured the same cold, isolation, and poverty as did the men who tended lights. Without them, Canada and the United States could not have grown and prospered as they did. Without them, many of the millions of immigrants who sought the promise of the New World might never have reached these shores safely.

BEAVERTAIL LIGHT

Conanicut Island, Rhode Island – 1749 and 1856

North America's third lighthouse, after the Boston and Brant Point lights, was built at Beavertail Point on Conanicut Island south of Jamestown in 1749. Officials of the Rhode Island colony felt that the light was needed to guide ships around the point and into Newport Harbor or Narragansett Bay.

Conanicut Island was already famous for its association with Captain William Kidd, known to some as a privateer and, to the people he robbed, as a pirate. During the late 1600s Captain Kidd frequented the island, using it as an impromtu hideout. Some say he buried a substantial treasure here. If the treasure exists, it has never been found, but Kidd himself was found. Lured to Boston by Governor Bellomont, a former friend, Kidd was captured and eventually hanged in London.

During the Revolutionary War the British treated Beavertail Light almost as roughly as they had dealt with Captain Kidd many years before. In the summer of 1775, the British sailed into Newport Harbor and, when they left four years later, burned the Beavertail Lighthouse. The rubblestone tower survived the burning, but it was not fully repaired and back in operation until 1790.

The current square granite tower was built in 1856. Its fourth-order Fresnel lens flashes a green light eight times each minute from a height of sixty-four feet above the sea.

During the mid-1800s the station had a one-horse-power fog signal. Whenever fog or heavy weather set in, the keeper walked his trusty old nag on a treadmill that provided pressure for the horn.

HOW TO GET THERE:

From the east side of the Newport Bridge on Route 138, take East Shore Road through Jamestown and follow signs to Beavertail State Park. This historic lighthouse is a "must visit," especially for those who enjoy watching ocean waves crash against rocks.

In Rhode Island, it is possible to visit or at least see several lighthouses in one day. The square-towered Dutch Island Light, a Narragansett Bay light station established in 1826 and inactive since 1947, can be seen from a camping area south of Jamestown. Plum Beach Light, a caisson-style or spark-plug lighthouse, built in 1897 and deactivated in 1941, can be seen from the Jamestown Bridge.

The square granite tower of Beavertail Lighthouse rises above the southern end of Rhode Island's Conanicut Island. British redcoats burned an earlier lighthouse here during the Revolutionary War.

POINT JUDITH LIGHT

Point Judith, Rhode Island – 1810, 1816, and 1857

One of several dangerous coastal areas known to sailors as the "graveyard of the Atlantic," Point Judith has threatened mariners with its shoals since the first European ships arrived to explore these shores. The point, which thrusts several miles out into the Atlantic, is especially menacing in a storm. As early as the American Revolution, a beacon was maintained there to warn ships, but no lighthouse was built on the point until 1810. In that year the government hired contractor Daniel Way to construct a tower. A crude wooden structure, Way's tower was blown over by a gale in 1815.

By 1816 a second, sturdier lighthouse stood on the point. Its cylindrical walls, made of rough stone and cement, rose thirty-five feet above the ground and seventy-five feet above the sea. Driven by a clockwork mechanism powered by a 288-pound weight, the lamps and lenses rotated on a copper table so that sailors saw a flash every two and a half minutes.

The Lighthouse Board ordered construction of the current Point Judith Lighthouse in 1857. Its octagonal granite-block tower stands sixty-five feet above the water, and its light, focused by a fourth-order Fresnel lens, has a range of sixteen miles. The light occults, or goes dark briefly, every fifteen seconds.

Despite the presence of a light on Point Judith, its shoals have continued to destroy ships. The *Normandy* (1864), *American Eagle* (1870), *Acusionet* (1870), *Venus* (1877), *Cucktoo* (1882), *Harry Barry* (1888), *Anita* (1888), *Mars* (1892), *Blue Jay* (1896), *Amanda E.* (1902), *Comet* (1973), and countless other vessels have been lost nearby.

On some early maps the area is marked as "Point Juda Neck." Perhaps that is how it got its current name. But, according to an often-told, whimsical story, the point was given its name by an old, nearsighted captain whose daughter Judy was the first aboard his small vessel to spot the point. Unable to see the land himself, the captain cried out, "Point, Judy!"

HOW TO GET THERE:

From U.S. 1, drive south on Route 108 to the Coast Guard Station at Point Judith. Strewn with rocks and pebbles polished by the surf, the beaches here are very beautiful.

Point Judith Light shines over one of the most dangerous stretches of North America's Atlantic coast. Killer storms and shoals, lurking just beneath the surface, have destroyed countless ships within sight of this light.

WATCH HILL LIGHT

Watch Hill, Rhode Island – 1807 and 1855

The people of Rhode Island built a watchtower on strategic Watch Hill during King George's War (1744–48). Its purpose, however, was not to guide ships but rather, to provided early warning of a naval attack. No such attack came, and the tower fell into ruin. A gale wiped away all traces of the watchtower in 1781.

Although the importance of Watch Hill as a mark for vessels moving in and out of Block Island Sound was widely recognized, no lighthouse was built here until the early nineteenth century. In 1806 the Lighthouse Service hired Elisha Woodward of New London, Connecticut, to built a round wooden tower and protect its walls with shingles. A bank of ten whale-oil lamps provided the light.

In 1855, during the flurry of lighthouse construction started after the Lighthouse Board took charge of navigational aids, a new tower appeared on Watch Hill. Built with long, rectangular blocks of gray granite, it placed the focal plane of its light sixty-one feet above the sound.

Originally, the lantern displayed a fixed white light focused by a fourth-order Fresnel lens. But early in this century, when bright street lights began to compete with the lighthouse and confuse navigators, the lens was replaced with a rotating optic displaying a flashing white light every fifteen seconds.

HOW TO GET THERE:

Take Route 1A from Westerly to Watch Hill and park in the village. The light cannot be seen from the village, but it is just over the hill, and you can easily walk to it, although only the grounds are open to the public. The village offers several charming shops and restaurants.

Colonial soldiers once stood on a tower nearby here to watch for the sails of enemy ships. Nowadays sailors keep an eye out for the beacon of the Watch Hill Lighthouse.

LIGHTHOUSES OF BLOCK ISLAND

Block Island North – 1867

Block Island Southeast – 1875

Helmsmen give Block Island a wide berth. Ringed by submerged boulders and sandy shoals, the six-mile-long island has ended the careers of countless ships and no few sailors. In a single twenty-year stretch during the early 1800s, thirty-four schooners, fifteen sloops, eight brigs, and two larger ships wrecked on Block Island.

To cut these losses, the Lighthouse Service built a tower on Sandy Point, a finger of land pointing north toward Point Judith. Constructed at a cost of $15,000, the tower stood forty-five feet high; its light could be seen for twelve miles. The rapidly shifting sands of Sandy Point proved almost as liquid as the sea, however, and the lighthouse had to be rebuilt three times to pull it back from the encroaching ocean.

The current Block Island North (Sandy Point) Lighthouse, built in 1867, served for more than a century before it was deactivated and replaced in 1970 by an automated

offshore beacon. Somewhat resembling a church or schoolhouse, it was made of brownish-gray granite and had a brown, metal-walled lantern protruding from its roof. The lantern once housed a fourth-order Fresnel lens and cast over the water an occulting white light that could be seen from about thirteen miles away. Hiram Ball, who successfully promoted Block Island as a swank Victorian resort, also served for many years as the keeper of North Light. Ball could truthfully boast to the island's wealthy visitors that he had been appointed to the post by President Abraham Lincoln.

Ball was long gone from the North Light by February 1907, when the steamer *Larchmont* ran into the schooner *Henry Knowlton* just off the northwest coast of Block Island. The *Larchmont* got the worst of the collision and rapidly sank, dumping 150 passengers and crew into the freezing waters of Block Island Sound. Only nineteen of

For more than a century, the Block Island North Lighthouse guided sailors around a bank of deadly shoals. Renovated in 1993, the lighthouse draws many visitors.

those aboard the *Larchmont* survived. The *Knowlton* also sank, but more slowly, and its crew rowed to safety near the Watch Hill Light, several miles to the northwest.

Among the most remarkable structures in North America is the Block Island Southeast Lighthouse, built high on the Mohegan Bluffs in 1875. The sixty-seven-foot octagonal tower and attached Victorian-style keeper's duplex were constructed of red brick. Because of the considerable elevation of the bluffs, the lantern throws out its flashing green light from a point more than 200 feet above the water. The light is focused by a huge, first-order Fresnel lens fashioned by the Henry Lapaute Company of Paris for $10,000; its name is found on some of the brass fittings of the lens. The entire station cost the U.S. Treasury more than $75,000 to build, but the light's first keeper, Henry Clark, was paid only $600 a year to manage it.

Not far from the granite foundations of the lighthouse, cliffs drop sharply into the ocean more than 160 feet below. These cliffs must have seemed even loftier to the war party of fifty Mohegan Indians who were trapped here in 1590. The Mohegans, who were from Long Island, New York, appeared suddenly in their war canoes and launched a raid against the local Indians. But the Block Island warriors quickly defeated the invaders, drove them back to the bluffs, and threw them over the cliffs.

In 1993, the 2,000-ton Block Island Southeast Light was carefully moved 300 feet back from the sea. It was through the efforts of a dedicated group of volunteers that the necessary funds were raised.

Laced with Victorian charm, Block Island is well worth the long ferry ride from New London, Connecticut, or Galilee, Rhode Island. So are its lighthouses, both of which can be reached from the ferry slip by automobile, taxi, or bicycle. The Southeast Light stands just above the village on the Mohegan Bluffs. A visit to the inactive North Light, about six miles north of the village, requires a mile-long trek through deep sand. Thousands of seagulls flock in the area and are under the impression that the place belongs to them. When disturbed, they can make more noise and commotion than you might think possible.

HOW TO GET THERE:

For ferry schedules and reservations, call (203) 442–9553 in Connecticut or (401) 789–3502 in Rhode Island. For lighthouse information or to help with further restoration, write to the Block Island Southeast Foundation, P.O. Box 949, Block Island, RI 02807.

The perfect setting for a Victorian novel, Block Island Southeast Lighthouse commands a heavily eroded bluff. To keep the lighthouse safe, conservationists moved it inland (see inset) in 1993. (Inset courtesy International Chimney Corporation)

ROSE ISLAND LIGHT

Newport, Rhode Island – 1870

Among the most interesting of Rhode Island's lighthouses is the Rose Island Light near Newport. Built in 1870 on top of old Fort Hamilton, the station served for a century before the Coast Guard darkened its lantern in 1971. With a small tower rising from the mansard roof of a stone keeper's dwelling, it guided mariners sailing the lower reaches of Narragansett Bay. This light must have been a familiar sight to Ida Lewis, heroine and famed keeper of the Lime Rock Light in Newport Harbor (see page 83).

Construction of the Newport Bridge made the Rose Island Lighthouse obsolete. Towering over the lighthouse, the bridge served much more effectively as a navigational marker.

Abandoned by the Coast Guard, the old lighthouse had been nearly destroyed by vandalism and neglect before the nonprofit Rose Island Lighthouse Foundation undertook a determined campaign to save the structure in 1984. So successful were the work and fund-raising efforts of the foundation that the lighthouse has now been fully restored and relit as a private aid to navigation.

HOW TO GET THERE:

The lighthouse operates spring through fall as a museum. Public transportation by boat is available from Newport or Jamestown. Of particular interest to those seeking a unique experience, the Rose Island Lighthouse is open to evening guests all year as an inn. An overnight or weekend stay on Rose Island may give visitors a sense of what it was really like to be a lighthouse keeper. For boat schedules, inn reservations, or information, call (401) 847–4242.

For more than a century, the Rose Island Lighthouse, near Newport, Rhode Island, guided ships through the lower reaches of Narragansett Bay. Now it serves as a unique bed and breakfast.

It looks like a near miss, but the freighter Hercules is actually a safe distance from the Pomham Rocks Lighthouse, situated in the East Providence River. Unfortunately, this interesting structure is closed to the public and is very difficult to see from any convenient vantage point in Providence. You may catch a glimpse of it from Route 103.

NEW LONDON HARBOR LIGHT

New London, Connecticut – 1760 and 1801

The citizens of states in the U.S. Northeast are quite familiar with lotteries. Tickets for weekly cash-prize drawings can often be purchased in gas stations, small grocery stores, and sometimes even restaurants. Proceeds from the lotteries are usually used to pay for roads, bridges, schools, and similar projects. Colonial Americans also practiced this mild, civic-minded form of gambling. In fact, the people of New London, Connecticut, raised money for the town's first lighthouse with a lottery. No record remains of how much money the lottery raised, but it was enough to build a stone tower sixty-four feet high and twenty-four feet in diameter at the base. A ton-nage tax was imposed on shipping to pay the keeper and maintain the lighthouse. When the whale-oil lamps of the New London tower were first lit in 1760, only three other lighthouses marked the coasts of colonial America.

Unlike the Boston Light, the lighthouse at New London survived the Revolutionary War. In fact, American privateers used the beacon to help them find shelter from British warships. But while the light escaped the violence of the war, it did not long survive the ravages of wind and weather. By 1799 a ten-foot crack had opened in its walls, and the U.S. government decided to tear it down and rebuild. The new lighthouse, erected near the site of its predecessor, has proven far more durable. Built in 1801 for $15,547.90, the octagonal sandstone tower and separate keeper's dwelling still stand.

The tower rises ninety feet above an outcropping of rocks on the banks of the Thames River. Its lantern houses a fourth-order Fresnel lens focusing a 6,000-candlepower white light. A red sector in the light warns ships away from Sarah Ledge and other shoals to the west of the harbor.

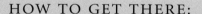

HOW TO GET THERE:

The grounds and keeper's dwelling are privately owned and closed to the public, but the lighthouse can be seen from Pequot Avenue, near Ocean Beach. Nearly two centuries old, the tower rises from a rocky outcropping on the west bank of the Thames River.

A few miles to the west of New London, just off I–95, is Mystic Seaport, an authentically restored nineteenth-century coastal village. The seaport boasts more than 300 antique vessels as well as its own lighthouse, a reproduction of the Brant Point Light on Nantucket. Although the lighthouse is not original, it does give visitors a sense of how harbor lights served seaman. With the high masts of the Charles W. Morgan and Joseph Conrad sailing ships in the background, it also provides a tempting opportunity for photographers. A fourth-order Fresnel lens is on display in the seaport's visitors' center.

New London lighthouses have weathered countless storms since 1760, when the first light here was built with money raised in a lottery. (© Thomas Hahn)

NEW LONDON LEDGE LIGHT

New London, Connecticut – 1909

This three-story mansion is located in a very exclusive neighborhood. There is room here for only one house. The "street" that runs in front of the mansion—and on all four sides—is Long Island Sound. Freighters, ferries, and pleasure craft sail by at all hours of the day and night. We must assume the designers of the New London Ledge Lighthouse had a sense of humor. Why else would they build a French Second Empire–style edifice on a submerged ledge at the entrance to New London Harbor? Perhaps no other lighthouse in North America seems so out of character with its surroundings.

Built in 1909 for $93,968, an astounding sum at the time, the Ledge Lighthouse was supposed to do what the New London Harbor Light could not do in fog and foul weather: warn ships away from the dangerous shoals near the mouth of the Thames River. The lantern, rising from the center of the roof like a cupola, once housed a fourth-order Fresnel lens that floated on a reservoir of mercury. A clockwork mechanism rotated the lens, causing the light to flash. The old lens, produced in Paris by Henry Lapaute, has been removed and replaced by a smaller automated lens. Sailors see three white flashes and then one red flash every thirty seconds.

Some say the lighthouse is haunted. During the 1930s the New London Ledge keeper's wife ran away with the captain of one of the Block Island ferries that passed by the lighthouse almost every day. The distraught keeper pushed open the steel lantern door and jumped to his death on the rocks below. Later keepers claimed they heard strange noises and footsteps, found the lantern door open when they were sure they had closed and bolted it, and felt "cold spots" in certain rooms. Now that the lighthouse is automated, the New London Ledge ghost, if there is one, must be very lonely.

HOW TO GET THERE:

This unique structure can be seen from several vantage points on Ocean Beach, on the south side of New London. Passengers on the Block Island Ferry, which operates from mid-June to Labor Day, enjoy a particularly fine view of the light. For ferry information, call (203) 442–7891.

LIGHTHOUSES OF THE CONNECTICUT SHORE

Five Mile Point – 1805 and 1840

Stonington Harbor – 1824 and 1840

Sheffield Island – 1826 and 1868

Like its neighbor Rhode Island, Connecticut is a friend of the sea. The typically calm waters of Long Island Sound form a highway for ships. Its proximity to heavily traveled shipping channels helped make Connecticut a successful colony and, after the Revolution, a prosperous state. Not surprisingly, Connecticut has lots of lighthouses, many of them dating back nearly two centuries.

Among the oldest and best known of these is the Five Mile Point (New Haven) Lighthouse, established in 1805. New Haven's first light tower was made of wood, but it was replaced by a more sturdy stone tower in 1840. Its light guided ships in and out of the New Haven Harbor until the lighthouse was decommissioned in 1877. Today it serves as the chief attraction of the city's Lighthouse Park.

The Stonington Harbor Lighthouse, built in 1824, first stood on Windmill Point. Erosion undercut the structure, and in 1840 the government had it torn down and rebuilt on the east side of the harbor. A thirty-five-foot stone tower with attached dwelling, this lighthouse was discontinued in 1889; but, like the Five Mile Point Lighthouse, it has miraculously survived the years. Today the Stonington Historical Society uses it as a museum.

Another lighthouse that has stood dark for nearly a century can be found on Sheffield Island in Norwalk. Established in 1826 and rebuilt in 1868, the gabled, two-story stone building served as a lighthouse until the turn of the century. Shortly after 1900 it was decommissioned. Restored and cared for by the Norwalk Seaport Association, the old lighthouse is now open to the public.

The octagonal stone tower of Five Mile Point Lighthouse has stood since 1840. Out of service for more than a century, the old tower has miraculously survived the ravages of time and urban growth. (© William Kaufhold)

Its lens removed long ago, the stubby stone tower of Stonington Harbor Lighthouse (left) still stands. Resembling a small New England country church, the Sheffield Island Lighthouse (right) is another historical survivor. (© William Kaufhold)

HOW TO GET THERE:

New Haven Lighthouse: *Take exit 50 off I–95 and follow Townsend Avenue (Route 337) south; then turn right onto Lighthouse Road. Lighthouse Park features not only the old lighthouse tower but also a nice beach.*

    Stonington Harbor Lighthouse: *Follow U.S. 1 east from New London to Stonington. Turn right onto Water Street and follow it through historic Stonington Village to its end at the lighthouse. Located in the venerable structure is the Old Lighthouse Museum, open 11:00 A.M. to 4:30 P.M. daily (except Monday) from May through October.*

    The **Sheffield Island Lighthouse** *is located on a scenic island that also contains a noted wildlife refuge. Together the lighthouse and Stewart McKinney National Wildlife Refuge make the island well worth a visit. Passage to Sheffield Island is available from Hope Dock in Norwalk. Take exit 14 off I–95 and follow Fairfield Avenue and then Washington Street. Turn left onto Water Street and look for the dock immediately on the right. For information on lighthouse cruise schedules and fares, call (203) 334–9166.*

BIBLIOGRAPHY

Adams, William Henry Davenport. *Lighthouses and Lightships: A Descriptive and Historical Account of Their Mode of Construction and Organization.* New York: Scribner, 1870.

Adamson, Hans Christian. *Keepers of the Light.* New York: Greenberg, 1955.

Beaver, Patrick. *A History of Lighthouses.* Secaucus, N.J.: Citadel, 1972.

Caldwell, Bill. *Lighthouses of Maine.* Portland, Me.: Gannett Books, 1986.

Frost, Walter S., and Harold G. Simms. *The Lighthouses of Maine: A Guide for Photographers and Artists.* Frost and Simms, 1980.

Hamilton, Harlan. *Lights and Legends: A Historical Guide to Lighthouses of Long Island Sound, Fishers Island Sound and Block Island Sound.* Stamford, Conn.: Wescott Core Publishing Co., 1987.

Holland, Francis Ross, Jr. *America's Lighthouses: Their Illustrated History Since 1716.* Brattleboro, Vt.: Stephen Greene Press, 1972.

Moe, Christine. *Lighthouses and Lightships.* Monticello, Ill.: Moe, 1979.

Putnam, George R. *Sentinel of the Coasts.* New York: Norton, 1937.

Scheina, Robert L. "The Evolution of the Lighthouse Tower." *In Lighthouses: Then and Now* (supplement to the U.S. Coast Guard Commandant's Bulletin).

Snow, Edward Rowe. *Famous Lighthouses of America.* New York: Dodd, Mead, 1955.

——. *Famous New England Lighthouses.* Boston: Yankee Publishing, 1945.

Sterling, R. T. *Lighthouses of the Maine Coast.* Brattleboro, Vt.: Stephen Daye Press, 1935.

United States Coast Guard. *Historically Famous Lighthouses.* CG–232, 1986.

——. *Chronology of Aids to Navigation and Old Lighthouse Service.* CG–485, 1974.

Weiss, George. *The Lighthouse Service: Its History, Activity and Organization.* Baltimore: Johns Hopkins University, 1926.

Welch, Wally. *The Lighthouses of Massachusetts.* Apopka, Fl.: Lighthouse Publications, 1989.

——. *The Lighthouses of Rhode Island.* Apopka, Fl.: Lighthouse Publications, 1987.

LIGHTHOUSES INDEX

Numerals in italics indicate photograph/legend only.

FOR FURTHER INFORMATION
ON LIGHTHOUSES

Block Island Southeast Lighthouse Foundation
P.O. Box 524
Block Island, RI 02807

Island Institute
P.O. 249
Rockland, ME 04843

Lighthouse Preservation Society
P.O. Box 763
Rockport, MA 01966

National Park Service, Division of History
Maritime Initiative
P.O. Box 37127
Washington, DC 20013

New England Lighthouse Foundation
P.O. Box 1690
Wells, ME 14090

Shore Village Museum
104 Limerock Street
Rockland, ME 04841

St. George Historical Society
Marshall Point Lighthouse Museum
P.O. Box 247
Port Clyde, ME 04855

Portland Head Lighthouse Museum
Town of South Portland
P.O. Box 252
Cape Elizabeth, ME 04107

United States Lighthouse Society
244 Kearney Street
5th Floor
San Francisco, CA 94108

U.S. Coast Guard, 1st District
408 Atlantic Avenue
Boston, MA 02210

PHOTO INFORMATION

The best time to photograph lighthouses is at dusk—the edge between day and night. The soft light that appears after the sun is below the horizon brings magic to color photos. The light in a tower appears brighter as the daylight fades; and as dusk comes on, a lighthouse is at its best. See pages 13, 42, 53, 67, and 74 for examples.

To capture this effect, use a tripod and slower shutter speeds. The pictures in this book were taken on Fuji 100 daylight film on a Nikon 8008 camera using either a wide-angle or telephoto lens. The dusk photo of Rockland Breakwater Lighthouse on page 42 was taken with a 300-mm telephoto lens set at f 4.5, and the shutter was open for a full-second exposure. Look at the photo on page 41, which was shot from a passing ferry in midmorning. There is a bit of mystery and mood at dusk that is not there during midday.

The photo of Pemaquid Point on page 46 was taken looking east just after sunset. The orange light of the setting sun was replaced by a softer light reflected off clouds in the western sky (behind the camera), but there was still enough light to shoot at a shutter speed of about $\frac{1}{10}$ of a second. You can tell how long the exposure was by looking at the movement in the waves. Longer exposures will blur the waves and turn them into a foggy countenance, which also makes interesting pictures. On pages 55 and 80, the harsh orange light of sunset has also faded into a more interesting and soft magenta light.

The picture of the Cape Elizabeth Light on page 53 was taken before the sunset but after the sun was low enough to be softened by a summer haze on the horizon. The long shadow under the eaves is the tip-off here. A 300-mm telephoto lens was used from a distance of about 100 yards to keep the vertical lines of the house looking straight—by not tilting the camera up. When a camera is tilted up, it makes the vertical lines tilt inward and often makes a building look as if it were falling over backward; a wide-angle lens will aggravate this look. Another way to prevent this amateur look is to put something interesting in the foreground and hold the camera level; see the examples on pages 34, 47, 55 (Cape Neddick with small red building and fence), and 92.

On page 80 the picture of Mystic Seaport Lighthouse was taken an hour after sunset, when all the color had faded from the sky and a deep blue night look fell on the film. Exposure here was about ten seconds, perhaps a bit longer. Daylight film will almost always give this deep blue just before total darkness in the sky. The trick here is not to wait until total darkness—you must have a smidgen of light to make it work.

Many of the photos were taken from a Cessna 172 light plane because it has a window that can be opened. Don't hold the camera outside, as the airstream will pull it and blur your photos; keep the lens just inside. The high-wing Cessna is best for these aerial photos because the wing is above the photographer. Shutter speeds of $\frac{1}{500}$ of a second prevent blur from the plane's speed. For this book, a short, 105-mm telephoto was used. See photos on pages 9, 21, 23, 27, 28, and 29.

Inside the lighthouse, a 24-mm wide-angle lens was used; see page 68. Lighthouses are grand subjects, but don't overlook a keeper's house. Sometimes the light will reflect in the window, and details and close-ups can produce totally unexpected pictures. See page 55.

—BRUCE ROBERTS

ABOUT THE AUTHORS

BRUCE ROBERTS and his wife, Cheryl, who helped with the research for this book, live on North Carolina's Outer Banks, not far from the Bodie Island Lighthouse. For many years Bruce was Senior Travel Photographer for *Southern Living* magazine. He started his career working as a photographer for newspapers in Tampa, Florida, and Charlotte, North Carolina. He is the recipient of many photography awards, and some of his photos are in the permanent collection of the Smithsonian Institution. Recently Bruce and Cheryl opened the Lighthouse Gallery & Gifts, a store devoted to lighthouse books, artifacts, and collectibles, in Nags Head.

RAY JONES is a freelance writer and publishing consultant living in Surry, a small town on the coast of Maine. He began his writing career working as a reporter for weekly newspapers in Texas. He has served as an editor for Time-Life Books, as founding editor of *Albuquerque Living* magazine, as a senior editor and writing coach at *Southern Living* magazine, and as founder and publisher of Country Roads Press. Ray grew up in Macon, Georgia, where he was inspired by the writing of Ernest Hemingway and William Faulkner, and worked his way through college as a disc jockey.